ELEMENTS
OF BIBLICAL
EXEGESIS

ELEMENTS OF BIBLICAL EXEGESIS

A Basic Guide for Students and Ministers

MICHAEL J. GORMAN

HENDRICKSON
PUBLISHERS

Copyright © 2001
Hendrickson Publishers, Inc.
P.O. Box 3473
Peabody, Massachusetts 01961–3473

Elements of Biblical Exegesis is a revised edition of *Texts and Contexts*, © 1994, 1998 Michael J. Gorman.

Printed in the United States of America

Second printing — April 2002

Library of Congress Cataloging-in-Publication Data

Gorman, Michael J., 1955–
    Elements of biblical exegesis: a basic guide for students and
ministers   /   Michael J. Gorman.
        p. cm.
    Includes bibliographical references.
    ISBN 1-56563-485-3 (pbk.)
    1. Bible—Criticism, interpretation, etc.   I. Title.

BS511.2 .G67 2000
220.6'01—dc21

                                                                00-067299

To my teachers and my students

Table of Contents

Acknowledgments.   ix

Introduction.   1

1. The Task.   7

2. The Text.   35

3. Survey *(The First Element)*   59

4. Contextual Analysis *(The Second Element)*
   The Historical and Literary Contexts
   of the Text   65

5. Formal Analysis *(The Third Element)*
   The Form, Structure, and Movement
   of the Text   75

6. Detailed Analysis of the Text *(The Fourth
   Element)*   91

7. Synthesis *(The Fifth Element)* 115

8. Reflection *(The Sixth Element)*
   The Text Today 123

9. Expansion and Refinement of the Exegesis
   (The Seventh Element). 135

10. Exegesis and the Exegete
    Errors to Avoid, Discoveries to Make 141

11. Resources for Exegesis. 147

Appendix A
A Chart of Exegetical Methods
Three Approaches 195

Appendix B
Practical Guidelines for Writing a Research
Exegesis Paper. 205

Appendix C
A Short Sample Exegesis Paper 211

Appendix D
A Longer Sample Exegesis Paper 217

Appendix E
Selected Internet Resources for
Biblical Studies 233

Index 237

Acknowledgments

I willingly acknowledge the input of others, especially my own teachers, in the development of the method described in this book. Among those who were especially formative were John Herzog, Gordon Fee, David Adams, Paul Meyer, and Bruce Metzger. Special thanks is due to the late Professor J. Christiaan Beker of Princeton Theological Seminary, whose clear procedure was surpassed only by the depth of the results obtained when he employed it. I am grateful to my former colleagues at the Council for Religion in Independent Schools who read the earliest manuscript and made helpful suggestions: Catherine Sands, the late Nancy Davis, and Daniel Heischman. I am also grateful to two friends from graduate school and teaching days at Princeton Seminary: Bart Ehrman, now of the University of North Carolina at Chapel Hill, and Duane Watson, of Malone College, each of whom reacted favorably to earlier versions of this book.

Likewise, I thank colleagues at St. Mary's Seminary and University who appreciated and made use of earlier forms of this book: Peter Culman of the homiletics department; Sr. Sarah Sharkey and Fr. Pat Madden, both formerly of the Scripture department; and Fr. Paul Zilonka and Steve McNeely, my current colleagues in New Testament. I owe a special debt of gratitude to Paul Zilonka, who carefully read every word of the manuscript in draft form and made many helpful suggestions. In addition, I am grateful to my colleagues in Hebrew Bible/Old Testament, Fr. Michael Barré,

Ed Hostetter, and David Leiter, who provided assistance in preparing the bibliography.

I am also grateful to my friends and colleagues at other institutions who constantly force me to think carefully about both how and why I read the Bible, and whose interpretive abilities, in many cases, are extraordinary. I acknowledge particularly Steve Fowl (Loyola College in Maryland) and Greg Jones (Duke Divinity School), both of whom have been colleagues with me in the Ecumenical Institute of Theology; Richard Hays and Stanley Hauerwas, both of Duke; Jim Brownson of Western Theological Seminary; and Frances Taylor Gench of Union Theological Seminary in Virginia. I of course do not hold them, or any of the other people mentioned in this book, responsible for my perspectives or for the execution of them in print or in the classroom. (Nor do I, of course, concur with each or any of them at every point along the way.)

I am especially grateful to my students at Princeton Theological Seminary and at St. Mary's Seminary and University (both the School of Theology and the Ecumenical Institute of Theology) for what they have taught me. Extra thanks goes to one of my students, Bill Garrison, who served as my research assistant throughout the writing of this book. He helped particularly with the bibliographical sections of the book and made a thorough critique of several drafts. His invaluable suggestions have improved both the content and the format. Seminarian George Gannon, my new research assistant, helped with the proofreading and indexing. Last but not least, very special thanks is due Annette Chappell and Bryan Lowe, two excellent students who both used early versions of the book and contributed their fine exegetical work to the final product.

Finally, I express gratitude to my editor at Hendrickson, Shirley Decker-Lucke. Her belief in the project and astute suggestions have contributed immensely to its completion.

Introduction

Father Robert Leavitt, the President-Rector of the institution I serve, is an avid golfer with a three handicap. After he returned from a summer golf school at the famous Pebble Beach golf course in California, he surprised me by saying that his class included students of all abilities, from beginners to near-pros like himself. When asked how the instructors could meet the needs of such a diverse class membership, he responded, "They taught the basics." In fact, he said, that's what they do when PGA pros return to Pebble Beach for off-season instruction: they go back to the basics.

Preventing Exegetical Illiteracy

This book is about basics, about fundamentals. Designed for students, teachers, pastors, and others wishing to think and write about the Bible carefully, it began as a guide for seminary students learning to do careful analysis of the New Testament for classes, ordination exams, and preaching. First presented to classes and to study groups preparing for ordination exams in the Presbyterian Church (some of whom had failed their first attempt at the exam, usually because they lacked a clear method!), the material proved to be a simple-to-learn and helpful tool. It was then put down in writing as a brief hands-on guide to biblical exegesis.

In 1990 The Council for Religion in Independent Schools published a form of the guide as *Texts and Contexts: A Guide to Careful Thinking and Writing about the Bible*, which served many students in various settings. A revised edition, published first at St. Mary's Seminary and then by Wipf and Stock Publishers, served hundreds of students at St. Mary's Seminary and University, with much success.

This book is a thoroughly revised work, though the basic principles of the method have remained the same even as I have tried to incorporate new insights from the never-static field of biblical interpretation. I am told that students are still failing exegesis exams, and I know from personal experience that much of today's preaching still reveals ignorance of the basic principles of exegesis.

This book is offered, therefore, for use at several levels and in several ways. The concepts and method are understandable to beginning Bible students in colleges, universities, pretheology programs, and seminaries. For these students, both the discussion of the method and the practice exercises at the end of each chapter are recommended. The book is useful as introductory or collateral reading in a course on the Bible or on any part of the Bible, or it can be given to students for independent reading and reference. Its use does not require, nor does it preclude, knowledge of the Bible's original languages.

For more experienced students and for ordained preachers, the discussion of a clear, logical method for studying the Bible may give them something they have not found elsewhere. Most biblical scholars use something like the method presented in this book in their own thinking, writing, and teaching, but I am afraid that this strategy is often not communicated methodically to students. My experience with pastors as well as seminary students has confirmed this hunch. Furthermore, many of the exegetical handbooks in print are too detailed and complex for most students and preachers to use on a regular basis. This book suggests how to read the biblical text carefully, whether one is preparing to discuss a passage in class, write an exegetical paper, or venture into the pulpit. It can thus be used as a reference in classes or seminars in biblical studies, exegesis, or homiletics. For seasoned preachers, this book will not so much provide tips on how to preach the text but advice (or reminders) about how to read the text more responsibly.

Cautions

Three words of caution may be in order before we begin. First, although the elements or steps are simple, mastering this process is not easy. It requires hard work and trial and error—but the hard work will pay off.

Second, I do not want to create the impression that I believe the method presented in this book is the only way to think and write about the Bible. There are many other ways that can be used by the modern interpreter. The method presented here is for the basic but careful historical, literary, and theological analysis of a relatively short text, though its principles can apply to reading Scripture (and almost anything else) in general. The method presented here is chosen as the starting place by a wide variety of readers; it can also be useful to those who wish to supplement it with other interpretive strategies.

Third, therefore, this book is not intended to replace more detailed books on interpretation of the Bible, on specific literary genres, or on hermeneutics. I am convinced, however, that the already difficult task of biblical exegesis and interpretation is becoming so complex, with the unending array of new methods and methodologies (not to mention new historical discoveries), that many students and preachers are tempted to abandon any hope of being "scholarly" or even careful in their reading and use of the Bible. When that happens, students and preachers—not to mention the houses of worship and the general public—will (and do) suffer immense losses. This book is *deliberately* basic, not to curtail further study but to stimulate it and, in the meantime, to prevent disaster in the classroom and the pulpit. My agenda, therefore, is quite simple and straightforward: to help prevent exegetical illiteracy among everyday readers, teachers, and preachers of biblical texts.

Readers will notice that the length of the chapters varies considerably in proportion to the nature of the topic under consideration. The chapter on "detailed analysis," for example, is much longer than the very short chapter on "survey." Readers will also notice that both sample exegesis papers, written by two of my students, are based on New Testament texts. That is solely because New Testament is the area in which I teach.

Suggestions for Teachers

1. It is beneficial to have students work through the entire text, both readings and exercises.

2. The book can be used in an introductory unit in a biblical studies course. Perhaps assign one section of the method, including at least one of the suggested exercises and the appropriate section on resources for expanding and refining that step, per class. This results in a base unit of about eight classes for the students to work through the method. Then allow ample time for writing a draft and final copy of an exegetical paper, perhaps in conjunction with the main biblical books read in the course. Alternatively, the book can also be spaced out over a longer period of time, integrated with the course content.

3. Encourage students to think for themselves as they read the Bible. Emphasize the fact that all students, no matter what their background, can make a valuable contribution to the group's understanding of the Bible. One way to stress this is to assign a nonbiblical text, such as a newspaper editorial or excerpt from a historical document, for individual or class "exegesis" before beginning the study of the Bible.

4. Devote extra time to any section of this book that especially perplexes your students and, of course, to any section that *you* deem particularly important for your students. In my own view, the material on historical and literary contexts and on form, structure, and movement are the most crucial for students to grasp.

5. In class, you may wish to have students discuss, and even defend, their answers to the exercises. If time permits, do additional exercises together in class. The more students practice, the better their exegetical work will be.

6. Have students read the sections of the sample exegesis papers that correspond to each assignment, but only *after* reading the "theory" and doing the exercises themselves.

7. When assigning exegetical papers, start small, with perhaps an essay of three to four pages (750–1,000 words). Students may eventually be encouraged to write a substantial paper of 2,000–3,000 words or more, depending on the level of the course.

CHAPTER ONE

The Task

"Take up and read, take up and read."
—*A child at play, overheard by Augustine,*
according to the Confessions *VIII, 12*

"And now the end has come. So listen to
my piece of advice: exegesis, exegesis,
and yet more exegesis!"
—*Karl Barth, in his farewell to his students*
before his 1935 expulsion from Germany[1]

What is exegesis?

Whether you are reading the Bible for the first time or you have been reading it since early childhood, there will be passages that seem nearly impossible to understand. There will also be passages that you *think* you understand but that your instructors, classmates, fellow church members, or parishioners interpret quite differently. These kinds of experiences occur when people read any kind of literature, but we become particularly aware of them when we read *religious* literature—literature that makes claims on us. As we know, the Bible is the all-time bestseller, a book read, interpreted,

---

[1] Eberhard Busch, *Karl Barth: His Life from Letters and Autobiographical Texts* (Philadelphia: Fortress, 1976), quoted in Gordon D. Fee, *New Testament Exegesis: A Handbook for Students and Pastors* (rev. ed.; Louisville: Westminster John Knox, 1993), frontispiece.

and quoted by millions of people in countless ways. It would be easy to abandon any hope of understanding the Bible with some degree of confidence.

Such despair, however, is unnecessary. Although there are many approaches to the Bible, there is also a fair amount of common ground among responsible readers of the Bible. The purpose of this small book is to help you read, think about, and write about the Bible carefully and systematically using some of these common strategies. Although it is useful for the study of a portion of the Bible of any size, it is designed primarily for intense, precise study of a small section—a brief narrative, psalm, lament, prophetic oracle, speech, parable, miracle story, vision, or chapter-length argument, etc.—most of which consist of no more than several closely connected paragraphs. The technical term for such careful analysis of a biblical text is *exegesis*, from the Greek verb *exēgeisthai* meaning "to lead out" (*ex*, "out" + *hēgeisthai*, "to lead"). In this chapter we consider the task of exegesis and survey the method proposed in this book.

Exegesis as Investigation, Conversation, and Art

Exegesis may be defined as the careful historical, literary, and theological analysis of a text. Some would call it "scholarly reading" and describe it as reading in a way that "ascertains the sense of the text through the most complete, systematic recording possible of the phenomena of the text and grappling with the reasons that speak for or against a specific understanding of it."[2] Another appropriate description of exegesis is "close reading," a term borrowed from the study of literature. "Close" reading means the deliberate, word-by-word and phrase-by-phrase consideration of all the parts of a text in order to understand it as a

---

[2] Wilhelm Egger, *How to Read the New Testament: An Introduction to Linguistic and Historical-Critical Methodology* (ed. Hendrikus Boers; trans. Peter Heinegg; Peabody, Mass.: Hendrickson, 1996), 3.

whole. Those who engage in the process of exegesis are called exegetes.[3]

Many people over the years have understood the goal of exegesis to be the discovery of the biblical writer's purpose in writing, or what is called the "authorial intention." While a laudable goal, this is often difficult to achieve. Many interpreters today reject authorial intention as the goal of exegesis. It can be hard enough to grasp our own intentions in writing something, let alone those of another person from another time and culture. A more modest and appropriate primary goal would be to achieve a credible and coherent understanding of the text on its own terms and in its own context. Even that goal is a difficult one. This primary objective is often, though not always, pursued with a larger (and ultimately more important) existential goal—that somehow the text in its context may speak to us in our different-yet-similar context.

Exegesis is therefore an *investigation*. It is an investigation of the many dimensions, or textures, of a particular text. It is a process of asking questions of a text, questions that are often provoked by the text itself. As one of my professors in seminary used to put it, the basic question we are always asking is, "What's going on here?" In some ways, that question is enough, but it will be helpful to "flesh it out," to give this basic question some greater form and substance. Exegetes must learn to love to ask questions.

To engage in exegesis is to ask historical questions of a text, such as "What situation seems to have been the occasion for the writing of this text?" Exegesis also means asking literary questions of the text, such as "What kind of literature is this text, and what are its literary aims?" Furthermore, exegesis means asking questions about the religious, or theological, dimensions of the text, such as "What great theological question or issue does this text engage, and what claims on its readers does it make?" Exegesis means not being afraid

---

[3] However, exegetes should resist the temptation to create a new verb "to exegete," as in "to exegete a text."

of difficult questions such as "Why does this text seem to contradict that one?" Finally, exegesis means not fearing discovery of something new or puzzlement over something apparently insoluble. Sometimes doing exegesis means learning to ask the right questions, even if the questions are not immediately resolved. In fact, exegesis may lead to greater ambiguity in our understanding of the text itself, of its meaning for us, or both.

It would be a mistake, however, to think that we are the first or the only people to raise these questions of the biblical text as we seek to analyze and engage it carefully. Exegesis may also be defined as a *conversation*. It is a conversation with readers living and dead, more learned and less learned, absent and present. It is a conversation about texts and their contexts, about sacred words and their claims. As conversation, exegesis entails listening to others, even others with whom we disagree. It is a process best carried out in the company of other people through reading and talking with them—carefully, critically, and creatively—about texts. The isolated reader is not the ideal biblical exegete.

Nevertheless, we often read the Bible alone whether by choice or by virtue of our "profession." Students are normally required to write exegesis papers on their own. Pastors or other ministers usually prepare and preach sermons or homilies, grounded in careful study of the text, on their own. Whatever outside resources students or ministers may or may not consult, they need a method for the careful study of their chosen or assigned text. They need a way to enter the ongoing conversation about this or that text with confidence and competence, so that they too may contribute to the conversation. Hence the need for an exegetical method.

The word *method,* however, should not be equated precisely with "scientific method" or "historical method." Good reading—like good conversation or any sort of good investigation—is an art more than it is a science. Exegesis, as we will see throughout this book, is therefore an *art.* To be sure, there are certain principles and steps to follow, but knowing what to ask of a text, what to think about a text, and what to say about a text can never be known with complete certainty or done with method alone. Rather, an exegete needs not only principles, rules, hard work, and research skills, but also intuition, imagination, sensitivity, and even a bit of serendipity on occasion. The task of exegesis requires, therefore, enormous intellectual and even spiritual energy.

Exegesis, then, is investigation, conversation, and art. As conversation and art, exegesis requires an openness to others and to the text that method alone cannot provide. However, without a method, exegesis is no longer an investigation. Thus the principal focus of this book is on developing an exegetical method.

Choosing an Approach to the Task

Handbooks on "studying the Bible" and on "exegetical method" are plentiful. Some are simplistic, others incredibly complex. The method of exegesis presented in the following pages is neither. It may be similar to methods you have learned for reading and writing explications of poetry or other literature. For example, as a student of French in high school and college, I learned how to examine French literature closely, just as students in France do. The process and result was called an *explication de texte*. As noted above, this way of careful reading of a small portion of literature is sometimes known as "close reading." If you have never learned such a method, this book will also help you to be a more careful reader of literature in general.

The approach to exegesis advocated in this book is grounded in the conviction that we can read a text responsibly only if we attempt to understand the unique setting (historical context) in which it was produced and in which it is situated (literary context). Furthermore, we can understand a text only if we pay careful attention both to the whole and the parts (details), the proverbial forest as well as the trees. Before considering in detail the approach to exegesis proposed in this book, we need to understand something about the options available. In order to do that, we must become familiar with some rather technical terms.

Exegesis can be, in fact, a very technical field of inquiry. Interpreters of the Bible employ a variety of general approaches and specific methods to understand and engage the text. Some of these methods are called *criticisms*. The use of the term *criticism*, as in *redaction criticism*, does not necessarily imply negative judgment; the primary meaning of the term is *analysis*, though it may also mean judgment— whether negative, positive, or both—about the historical, literary, or theological value of a text.

There are perhaps three basic approaches to exegesis today. We will call them *synchronic, diachronic*, and *existential*.

THE SYNCHRONIC APPROACH

One approach to exegesis is called *synchronic* (meaning "with[in] time," i.e., "same time"; cf. "synchronize"). It may be compared to a cross section of a plant's stem in a biology textbook. This approach looks only at the final form of the text, the text as it stands in the Bible as we have it. It is not interested in the "long view" or "prehistory" of the text— any oral traditions, earlier versions, or possible written sources (such as the hypothetical sources called J, E, D, and P in the Pentateuch or Q in the gospels). Rather, the synchronic approach uses methods designed to analyze the text itself and the text in relation to the world in which it first existed as a text. The most common labels for this approach are narrative-critical, social-scientific, and socio-rhetorical. Socio-rhetorical criticism, for example, may be defined as an approach that "integrates the ways people use language with the ways they live in the world."[4]

This book will devote significant attention to synchronic methods of exegesis, but without a lot of the technical language that sometimes accompanies the discussion of these methods. They include:[5]

---

[4]Vernon K. Robbins, *Exploring the Texture of Texts: A Guide to Socio- Rhetorical Interpretation* (Valley Forge, Pa.: Trinity, 1996), 1.

[5]For a more inclusive overview of the various criticisms and the questions they seek to answer, see the chart in Appendix A.

- **literary criticism**—the quest to understand the text as literature by employing either traditional or more recent models of literary criticism that are employed in the study of literature generally; corollaries of literary criticism are **genre and form analysis,** the quests to classify a text as to its type.

- **narrative criticism**—as a subset of literary criticism, the quest to understand the formal and material features of narrative texts (stories) or other texts that have an implicit or underlying narrative within or behind them.

- **rhetorical criticism**—the quest to understand the devices, strategies, and structures employed in the text to persuade and/or otherwise affect the reader, as well as the overall goals or effects of those rhetorical elements (rhetoric is the art of effective communication).

- **lexical, grammatical, and syntactical analysis**—the quest to understand words, idioms, grammatical forms, and the relationships among these items according to the norms of usage at the time the text was produced.

- **semantic or discourse analysis**—the quest to understand the ways in which a text conveys meaning according to modern principles and theories of linguistics.

- **social-scientific criticism**—the quest for the social identity, perceptions of the world, and cultural characteristics of the writers, readers/hearers, and communities suggested by the text (the questions asked and/or methods used are often those of the social sciences, such as sociology and anthropology); usually divided into two distinct subdisciplines, **social description** and **social-scientific analysis.**[6]

---

[6] Some scholars would suggest that "social-scientific criticism" is not truly a synchronic method but is rather a new approach to traditional questions of historical criticism (described below as a diachronic method), which has been concerned broadly with the historical genesis and context ("background") of biblical documents. For our purposes, we may say that the primary difference between the two criticisms is one of emphasis, whether on describing and analyzing the social setting contemporary with the biblical text (social-scientific criticism) or on reconstructing the historical developments that led to the production of the biblical text (historical criticism).

If these terms and the methods to which they refer seem at first foreign or complex, readers should bear in mind that they have probably already been introduced to them in the study of literature. The synchronic approach to the text is quite similar to the way in which literary critics analyze a poem or other short text. Literary critics, when explicating a poem, for example, may consider the following features of it:

- **genre and implied situation**—the type of literature the text is, and the life situation implied by the text

- **intellectual core**—the topic and theme ("slant") of the text

- **structure and unity**—the arrangement of the text

- **literary** (e.g., poetic) **texture**—the details of the text

- **artistry**—the beauty of the text[7]

As we will see, these are all very similar to the elements of exegesis presented in this book. Many advocates of a primarily synchronic approach to texts also incorporate some of the methods of diachronic exegesis discussed below.

A synchronic approach to the Sermon on the Mount (Matthew 5–7) might ask questions such as the following:

- What are the various sections of the Sermon, and how do they fit together to make a literary whole?

- What does the narrator of this gospel communicate by indicating the setting of the Sermon, the composition of the audience before and after the Sermon, and the audience's reaction to it?

- What is the function of the Sermon in the gospel's portrayal of Jesus and of discipleship?

- How would a first-century reader understand and be affected by this Sermon?

---

[7] Adapted from Leland Ryken, *Words of Delight: A Literary Introduction to the Bible* (2d ed.; Grand Rapids: Baker, 1992), 207–11. Similarly, the basic standard parts of an *explication de texte* in French literature are situation, form, subject, analysis, and conclusion.

The Diachronic Approach
(The Historical-Critical Method)

The second approach to exegesis is the *diachronic* (meaning "across time") approach, and it focuses on the origin and development of a text, employing methods designed to uncover these aspects of it. It takes the "long view" of a text and may be compared to a longitudinal perspective on a plant stem in a biology text. As a constellation of methods, this approach is often referred to as the *historical-critical method*, and it was the approach of choice by many, if not most, biblical scholars of the twentieth century. It should be noted, however, that there is no consensus as to the scope and goals of this method.

This book will give some, but limited, attention to the so-called historical-critical methods of exegesis. They include:[8]

- **textual criticism**—the quest for the original wording of the text (and the ways later scribes altered it).

- **historical linguistics**—the quest to understand words, idioms, grammatical forms, and the relationships among these items, often with attention to their historical development within a language.

- **form criticism**—the quest for the original type of oral or written tradition reflected in the text, and for determining out of what sort of situation such a tradition might have developed.

- **tradition criticism**—the quest for understanding the growth of a tradition over time from its original form to its incorporation in the final text.

- **source criticism**—the quest for the written sources used in the text.

- **redaction criticism**—the quest for perceiving the ways in which the final author of the text purposefully adopted and adapted sources.

---

[8] For an overview of the various criticisms and the questions they seek to answer, see the chart in Appendix A.

- **historical criticism**—the quest for the events that surrounded the production of the text, including the purported events narrated by the text itself.[9]

A diachronic approach to the Sermon on the Mount might ask questions such as the following:

- What written or oral sources did the evangelist (gospelwriter) adopt, adapt, and combine to compose this "Sermon"?

- What are the various components of the Sermon (beatitudes, prayers, parables, pithy sayings, etc.), and what is their origin and development in Jewish tradition, the career of the earthly Jesus, and/or the life of the early church?

- What does the evangelist's use of them reveal about his theological interests?

- To what degree do these teachings represent the words or ideas of the historical Jesus?

There are some critics of the diachronic method who want to retain its historical emphasis but find the presuppositions of some of its practitioners (e.g., those who deny the possibility of miracles or the role of God's Spirit in the production of the Bible) inappropriate for the study of Scripture. They might propose a modified historical-critical method, one that accepts some of the goals of the method but not its "alien" aspects. One such scholar has proposed using the term "historical biblical criticism."[10]

Practitioners of the diachronic approach are also interested in some of the questions raised by advocates of a more

---

[9] I am using the term "historical criticism" in a rather general way to encompass the investigation of what has often been called the "occasion" of a document's writing as well as any other historical events related to the genesis, development, production, and background of the text under investigation. In this sense, as indicated in an earlier note, "historical criticism" and "social-scientific criticism" are closely related but differ in emphasis.

[10] Karl P. Donfried, "Alien Hermeneutics and the Misappropriation of Scripture," in *Reclaiming the Bible for the Church* (ed. Carl E. Braaten and Robert W. Jenson; Grand Rapids: Eerdmans, 1995), 19–46, esp. 22–25.

synchronic approach to the text. They may, for example, combine rhetorical criticism with more traditional historical-critical methods. Indeed, few exegetes today are "pure" practitioners of a diachronic approach.

The focus of investigation in both the diachronic and the synchronic approaches to the text is twofold: the world *of* or *within* the text and the world *behind* the text. That is, exegetes who investigate the text with these methods are literary and historical critics—analysts of the historical and literary features of the text. There is clearly some overlap in the two approaches. For example, practitioners of both approaches are interested in the historical or social contexts in which texts come to life and in the kind of literature texts are. But these are not the only possible focal points of investigation of a text. Some readers want to focus on the world *in front of* the text, the world that the text "creates."

THE EXISTENTIAL APPROACH

A third approach, which has no commonly used name, may perhaps be labeled *existential*. Since it is an increasingly common but also frequently criticized approach to exegesis,[11] we will consider it now in more detail than the others

---

[11] Choosing an appropriate label for this approach is extraordinarily difficult, and none is completely satisfactory. Other options, all of which have problems of their own, include *hermeneutical, instrumental, transformative, self-involving, pragmatic,* and *interactive.* Two points of clarification about the term used, and the concept it represents, are in order. (1) By using the term *existential,* I do not mean to make any connection to existentialism as a philosophy or to identify this approach exclusively with the specific *existentialist* interpretation of the Bible associated with the name of Rudolf Bultmann. I especially differentiate this approach to exegesis from the very individualistic emphasis found in Bultmann. (2) Some practitioners of exegesis more narrowly understood would argue that existential exegesis is not exegesis at all but *interpretation,* or *hermeneutics* (the technical term for interpretation). This argument often incorrectly assumes that diachronic (and perhaps also synchronic) approaches are objective

noted above, which are thoroughly discussed in many hand-books[12] and which will be considered as part of the exegetical procedure outlined in subsequent chapters.

Proponents of the existential approach to reading the Bible are primarily interested not in the text per se—whether understood in terms of its formation (diachronically) or its final form (synchronically)—but in the text as something to be engaged. Existential methods are therefore "instrumental" methods: they allow the text to be read as a means to an end, not as an end in itself. The end, or goal, of this kind of reading is often an encounter with a reality beyond the text to which the text bears witness. This "something beyond" may be a set of relations among people, a "spiritual" truth beyond the "literal" truth, God, and so on. The desired encounter may be either to embrace or to resist the reality, depending on the nature of the reality perceived and encountered. Those who approach the text fundamentally to encounter God through the mediation of the text may refer to this approach as *transformative*.

More generally, we may describe this approach to exegesis as *self-involving;*[13] readers do not treat the text as a historical or literary artifact but as something to engage experientially—something that could or should affect their lives. The text is taken seriously with respect to human existence

---

or scientific while existential readings are biased. In fact, however, all reading is biased, and the methods chosen affect both what is observed and which conclusions are drawn. Moreover, this third approach to exegesis has likely been the main one used by the majority of Bible readers throughout history, with the possible exception of some professional biblical scholars of the last two centuries or so. Its legitimacy is, nonetheless, still questioned by some professional theologians and biblical scholars, while others advocate it vigorously.

[12] See chapter 11, section 1, pp. 148–55, "Resources for Understanding the Task."

[13] For a use of this concept that rescues it from the privatistic inclinations of existentialism, see Anthony C. Thiselton, *New Horizons in Hermeneutics* (Grand Rapids: Zondervan, 1992), 272–307, 564–66, and 615–18.

now, both individual existence and life in community (the private self and the corporate self). The reader wants to engage not merely the world behind the text or the world of the text but the world *before* the text. Powerful texts in general, and religious texts in particular, have the ability to create an alternative world and to invite their readers to engage it.

In a very important way, existential readers enlarge the contexts within which the biblical text is read:[14]

- **canonical criticism**—exegesis is done in the context of the Bible as a whole

- **theological exegesis** and **spiritual reading**—exegesis is done in the context of a specific religious tradition and for religious purposes

- **embodiment** or **actualization**—exegesis is done in the context of attempting to appropriate and embody the text in the world

- **advocacy criticism, liberationist exegesis,** and **ideological criticism**—exegesis is done in the context of the struggle for justice or liberation

These contexts significantly affect the methods, goals, and results of exegesis.

This approach to the text might ask the following kinds of questions of the Sermon on the Mount:

- To what kind of contemporary faith and practice does the Sermon call contemporary readers?

- How might the text about "turning the other cheek" be a potential source of difficulty or even oppression for the politically or socially downtrodden?

- Does love of enemies rule out the use of resistance or violence in every situation?

- What spiritual practices are necessary for individuals and churches to live the message of the Sermon in the contemporary world?

---

[14] For an overview of some existential methods, see the chart in Appendix A, pp. 202–3.

Readers who approach the text in this way use diverse methods and have a wide variety of goals or agendas. Both
diachronic and synchronic methods can be appropriated,
and others may be introduced as well. Practitioners of existential exegesis judge the adequacy of any specific method
on the basis of its ability to assist in achieving the overall
goal of exegesis. This goal may be described as something
rather general, such as transformation or spiritual formation, or as something more specific, such as liberation or an
encounter with God.

Excursus: Some Types of Existential Exegesis

Existential approaches to the biblical text can be divided into
two basic types, those that operate with a fundamental trust in
or consent to the text, and those that operate with a basic suspicion of the text.

Trust/Consent

The most ancient existential approach is that of *theological
exegesis,* which is currently undergoing a great revival. Practitioners of theological exegesis read the text primarily as a
reliable vehicle of, source of, or witness to God's revelation
and will, which are discerned especially in communal reading
and conversation. The biblical text is read as a means of religious formation, both attitudinal and behavioral. In reading
the text, readers encounter God in some sense. This approach
may make use of any or all of the diachronic and synchronic
methods, but it also often involves expanding both the contexts within which the text is read and the kinds of methods
used. This is because the biblical text is understood as more
than a historical artifact or literary work; it is viewed as sacred
text, as Scripture.

Thus, for example, theological exegetes often practice some
form of *canonical criticism* by taking into account the canonical
context—the place of the text in the entire Bible as the religious
community's book—whereas a purely diachronic or historical-
critical approach would find that anachronistic (since the entire
Bible did not exist as one book when a particular biblical document was composed). Theological exegetes may also take into
account the perceived purposes of God in "salvation history,"

"the incarnation," or "the paschal mystery" (the death and resurrection of Jesus) as contexts for interpretation. They may also
appeal to tradition or "the rule of faith" (i.e., the framework of
orthodox belief) as the context for and guide to appropriate
exegesis.

Also, advocates of theological exegesis sometimes appeal to
premodern or *precritical* ways of Jewish and Christian reading of
the Bible that allow for a variety of meanings in the text. The
additional ways, which may include allegorical reading, yield
meanings that are sometimes referred to as spiritual rather than
literal meanings.[15] The current revival of interest in the so-called
"fourfold sense of Scripture" is especially important. This medieval way of reading the Bible insisted that scriptural texts had
(normally three) meanings in addition to the "literal" or "plain"
sense. Although the methods currently used differ from their
medieval counterparts, the questions asked by the methods are
the same: What are we to believe (faith), to expect (hope), and to
do (love)?[16]

A less academic variation of theological exegesis is the ancient
and revered practice of spiritual reading, or *lectio divina* (literally, divine or sacred reading). In some circles this term may be
unfamiliar, but similar practices may be called devotional reading. *Lectio divina* is an approach to reading the Bible that uses
contemplation and meditation in the context of prayer to encounter God and God's word to the individual or community.
Since the goal of spiritual reading is contemplation and formation (spiritual growth), not information or analysis, exegetical
methods might seem superfluous. But they are not. Meditation

---

[15] It should be noted that some modern theological exegetes zealously advocate the overthrow of most modern, especially
historical-critical, approaches to the Bible in favor of premodern
or precritical exegesis. Such ancient methods (including, for example, allegorical reading of the text) had their appropriate
pride of place in their day, and they still have much to teach us. It
is unlikely, however, that we can return to premodern ways of
reading and ignore the contributions of modern scholarship.
Ironically, some advocates of precritical approaches employ very
modern philosophical understandings of language and meaning
to justify their rejection of modern critical methods.

[16] These correspond to the medieval interpretations usually
labeled allegorical, anagogical, and tropological.

on a text means "chewing on it"[17] and requires asking questions of the text that are similar to the ones asked by exegetes who use synchronic, and even some diachronic, methods. Finally, many recent approaches to the Bible stress that, since the ultimate goal of biblical exegesis is not information but transformation, true exegesis is accomplished only when individuals and communities engage in the *embodiment* or *actualization* of the text. The reading community, we might say, is to become a "living exegesis" of the text.

Suspicion

A quite different, and much more recent, existential approach is known as *ideological criticism*. Practitioners of ideological criticism see the text as a witness to relations of power that can be harmful, especially to certain groups of marginalized people. Often using recently developed social-scientific methods, they seek to uncover and eventually to disarm the relations of oppressive power that the text both signifies and sanctions. The text is read and then "un-read" as a means of naming and being freed from oppression.

Somewhere between theological and ideological exegesis, but usually embodying a spirit of suspicion, lies *advocacy criticism* and its most common manifestation, *liberationist exegesis*. This type of exegesis is often theological in that it may bring an ethical or theological goal and criterion to the process of reading: the thing advocated or the liberation sought is often, though not always, understood as God's purpose in self-revelation. Texts are judged by their perceived ability to liberate (or to be used more generally for advocacy) or not. Like ideological criticism, liberationist exegesis often draws on social-scientific methods and models and is concerned to name and address oppression.

The Approach of This Book

At this point, what can the average careful reader of the Bible do? The range of options can seem overwhelming.

---

[17] M. Robert Mulholland Jr., *Invitation to a Journey: A Road Map for Spiritual Formation* (Downers Grove, Ill.: InterVarsity, 1993), 114.

What we need is a model of exegesis that takes account of all these approaches but does not require a Ph.D. in biblical studies (or in history, sociology, and linguistics) to execute. We need a model that recognizes the common features of biblical texts as ordinary devices of human communication while also recognizing the importance of specific, "sacred" features of biblical texts.

The approach advocated in this book is somewhat of an eclectic and yet integrated one, drawing on the insights and methods of all of the three basic approaches mentioned above, but maintaining that there is no one "right" way. In fact, the approach of this book is compatible with all three clusters of methods in use today and can serve as a foundation for more detailed or sophisticated work that does stress one approach over the others.[18]

Nonetheless, of the three approaches, the first, or synchronic one, is predominant in this book for several reasons. The most important reason is that all exegetes, whether beginners or professionals, deal directly with the final form of the text. It is this text that readers read, preachers preach, and hearers hear. Another reason is that the other approaches may require a degree of either sophistication in critical historical and linguistic skills or theological perspective that not all readers possess. Finally, even those whose primary goal in reading the text of Scripture is spiritual reading, the formation of doctrine and practice, or liberation must read in a way that is attentive to the form and substance of the words and images of the text.

---

[18] For a comprehensive theoretical approach to interpretation that seeks to integrate all three of the basic approaches discussed here, see Sandra M. Schneiders, *The Revelatory Text: Interpreting the New Testament As Sacred Scripture* (2d ed.; Collegeville, Minn.: Liturgical, 1999), esp. 97–179. A similar holistic approach, with a more hands-on format, may be found in W. Randolph Tate, *Biblical Interpretation: An Integrated Approach* (Peabody, Mass.: Hendrickson, 1991).

The guidelines presented in this book rest on several assumptions. Chief among these is the assumption that the Bible must be read in its various contexts—those things that accompany, or go "with" (Latin *con*), the text itself. This assumption, and the method of interpretation it produces, attempts to take many factors into account:

- that the Bible is the work of many people, written over a period of more than one thousand years in many different specific historical situations (the historical, social, and cultural contexts);

- that every biblical passage is located within a larger work and that it contributes to the aims of that work (the literary and rhetorical contexts);

- that the Bible is part of humanity's expression of its thirst for meaning and value in life (the human context);

- that for Christians and Jews the Bible is a unique and authoritative revelation of and/or witness to God's activity in history (the biblical/canonical and religious contexts);

- that all readers of the Bible, no matter how novice or sophisticated, interpret the Bible from within their own social situations and worldviews, and these social and intellectual locations affect the ways in which they understand the Bible (the contemporary context).

Each of these contexts has significant impact on the interpretation of biblical texts, and the careful reader must be aware of all of them.

A corollary to the last assumption ought also to be noted here: because of each reader's own unique experiences and "location," he or she will have insight into the Bible that no one else will have. Each reader can learn to bring together literary and historical perspectives as well as personal experience to understand a written text in a way that is unique to that individual and that contributes to the ongoing conversation about the text. Although the isolated individual is not the ideal interpreter of Scripture, there can be no conversation without unique individuals contributing to the discussion.

At the same time, however, there are necessary safeguards to ensure that one's *ex*egesis of the Bible is not really *eis*egesis—reading *into* the text (the Greek *eis* meaning "into"). A sound exegetical method is one such safeguard. Other safeguards include both the basic tools of biblical knowledge and research (Bible dictionaries, maps, concordances, etc.) and the fruits of research and reflection produced by biblical scholars and other interpreters of the Bible (in commentaries, journal articles, etc.). These publications can answer basic questions (who? what? when? where?) during the initial exegetical process. For example, they will provide answers to such basic inquiries as "Who was Josiah?" or "What is a denarius?" More important, scholarly resources also verify, sharpen, and correct your work after you have done your own exegesis. Thus one important aspect of the exegetical process is the confirmation and correction of your own discoveries and insights, the refinement and expansion of your ideas through conversation and research.

An Overview of the Method

Thus far we have examined rationale and theory. The remainder of this book is devoted to the nuts and bolts of exegesis—the careful reading of and writing about the Bible. A close, careful reading or exegesis of a biblical passage requires a process. The process proposed in this book has seven basic elements; these are briefly outlined here and will be developed in more detail in subsequent chapters.

For purposes of *reading* a biblical text, the elements in this process cannot and should not always be followed slavishly; these steps are, rather, the necessary *elements* of a careful reading, or exegesis. (Thus the title of this book is *Elements of Biblical Exegesis*.) The actual process of reading and interpretation is more like a circle than an outline, as you move back and forth from part to whole, text to context, original meaning to contemporary relevance, and so on. This process is sometimes referred to as a "hermeneutical circle," hermeneutics being the art of interpretation. Interpretation is indeed more like a circular than a linear process; it has been described as a process of "going forward by circling around."[19] Another helpful analogy is that of weaving: exegesis is the weaving together of unique but interrelated strands or elements of a careful reading of the text. Nevertheless, it will be extremely beneficial to think carefully through each of the discrete elements of, or steps in, the method.

For purposes of *writing* about a biblical text (for example, an exegetical paper), the following method can be successfully used as it stands to yield high-quality written interpretations. It can also be altered according to the needs and wishes of individual students and instructors.

The seven elements of the method are:

- **survey**—preparation and overview

- **contextual analysis**—consideration of the historical and literary contexts of the text

- **formal analysis**—of the form, structure, and movement of the text

- **detailed analysis**—of the various parts of the text

- **synthesis**—of the text as a whole

- **reflection**—on the text today

- **expansion and refinement**—of the initial exegesis[20]

---

[19] Frederick C. Tiffany and Sharon H. Ringe, *Biblical Interpretation: A Roadmap* (Nashville: Abingdon, 1996), 68–69.

[20] Though the order of presentation may be different, the main elements of exegesis are very similar to the elements of close reading done by literary critics, as listed above: *genre and implied situation,* or what we have called analysis of *form* and consideration of the *historical and literary contexts; intellectual core,* or what we have called *synthesis; structure and unity,* or what we have called *structure* and *movement; literary* or poetic *texture,* or what we have called *detailed analysis; and artistry,* or something like our *reflection.* For a process similar to the one proposed in this book, though presented in a somewhat less technical way and in a different sequence, see Tiffany and Ringe, *Biblical Interpretation: A Roadmap.*

It is important to note that some exegetes would consider the element of reflection to be something supplemental to exegesis itself. They might suggest that any notion of personal or theological reflection on a text is unscientific at best and an invitation to eisegesis at worst. However, as Rudolf Bultmann, the great German biblical scholar of the first half of the twentieth century said, there is no exegesis without presuppositions.[21] We all come to the text with interests in it, maybe even an agenda. Biblical texts compel us to ask not only "What?" but "So what?" Historical and literary critics we may be, but we are also human beings seeking an encounter with truths and realities to which sacred texts point.

Refusing to consider responsible reflection on and with the text as an aspect of exegesis is shortsighted and unnecessary. Most exegetes have their eyes on "two horizons"—the horizon, or world, of the biblical text itself, and the horizon, or world, of their own personal and corporate experience. This is both normal and appropriate, though there are ways of engaging these two horizons that are more responsible than others. Exegetes who have no interest in the contemporary significance of biblical texts are, of course, free to refrain from reflection on them. Most people, however, even if they do not consider themselves religious, find it difficult to avoid reflecting on great literature, religious or otherwise. We do not have to be committed spiritual readers or liberation theologians to have this legitimate interest, but neither do we have to hide our religious commitments when we approach the text even in an academic setting.

---

[21] Rudolf Bultmann, "Is Exegesis without Presuppositions Possible?" in *Existence and Faith: Shorter Writings of Rudolf Bultmann* (trans. Schubert Ogden; New York: Meridian, 1960), 342–51. It has been pointed out by Anthony Thiselton (*New Horizons in Hermeneutics,* 45) that by "presupposition" Bultmann was referring to a "pre-understanding" as a relation in life to the subject matter of the texts, not merely to beliefs, and especially not to fixed beliefs or doctrines that allow for no alteration.

Some Observations on the Process

Three observations about executing this method as a whole are now in order. First, readers may enter the process of exegesis at any of the first six steps, including that of reflection on the contemporary context, but the process is not complete until all seven elements have been considered and all strands woven together. In an exegesis paper, these elements are carefully interconnected and presented systematically.

Second, the elements outlined here are fundamentally the same used by the majority of professional biblical scholars (although some hesitate to include element six, reflection) as well as literary critics. Although the work of biblical scholars and literary critics is more technical, as are the terms used to describe it (see Appendix A), scholars are basically asking the very questions about texts and their contexts that are raised by these seven elements.

Third, the reader of biblical texts who follows the basic process presented in this book can both contribute to the ongoing conversation about the Bible and benefit from that conversation. This last point implies something about the way in which students, preachers, and others proceed as they engage a text exegetically. The great temptation is to turn an exegesis paper into a research paper that lays out for the reader the major points of view on this or that passage, verse, or key word. Students who succumb to this temptation are often intimidated by the vast quantity and technical nature of biblical scholarship, especially in comparison to their own paucity of knowledge and skill. Then they make the mistake of thinking that, if they just read all the important commentaries and articles, they will finally understand the passage. Unfortunately, some instructors reinforce this notion.

It is much, much better for all readers—students, preachers, and other serious readers—to learn the habit of first reading the text largely on their own. Even the most sophisticated advocates and practitioners of the most complex historical-critical methods emphasize this:

> Before reaching for the secondary sources, such as the commentaries, one should try to formulate a provisional analysis of the text.[22]

By working through a text on your own, guided by a careful exegetical method, you will learn to engage the text itself, and not merely the interpreters or interpretations of the text. You will also be prepared to handle the biblical text responsibly in the absence of secondary sources. You will use secondary resources to expand, correct, and refine your own initial exegesis in a way that will enable you to learn from and contribute to the conversation about the text in your own unique ways more efficiently than those who begin with the interpretations of the text rather than with the biblical text itself.

For this reason, the last step in the exegetical process is called "Expansion and Refinement of the Exegesis." Although this is a discrete step in the exegetical process, it does not translate into a separate section of an exegesis paper. Rather, a paper should constantly, throughout each section of the paper, weave together one's own insights with the insights and corrective influences of others. Thus expansion and refinement of one's exegesis must occur for every element of the process.

In writing an exegesis paper that follows the elements of this process, a student must write precisely and concisely, for the process of investigation and conversation will uncover a lot of information about, and perspectives on, the text. Sometimes students are tempted to spend nearly half of their paper on contextual analysis, or on contextual and formal analysis, to the neglect of detailed analysis. While context and form are very important, they cannot replace careful, in-depth examination. The following general guidelines for a 15-page (approximately 4,000 words) exegesis paper may therefore be helpful:

---

[22] Hans Conzelmann and Andreas Lindemann, *Interpreting the New Testament: An Introduction to the Principles and Methods of N.T. Exegesis* (trans. Siegfried S. Schatzmann; Peabody, Mass.: Hendrickson, 1988), 38.

- **survey/introduction:** 1 page or less (approximately 250 words)

- **contextual analysis—historical and literary contexts:** 2–3 pages (approximately 500–800 words)

- **formal analysis—form, structure, and movement:** 1–2 pages (approximately 250–600 words)

- **detailed analysis:** 8–10 pages (approximately 2,000–2,750 words)

- **synthesis:** 1 page or less (approximately 250 words)

- **reflection:** 0–3 pages (0–approximately 750 words)

This is another way of saying that generally about one-half to two-thirds of the paper will be devoted to detailed analysis. Another way to imagine the paper is in three main parts: a "prelude" to the detailed analysis (steps 1–3), the detailed analysis itself, and a "postlude" (steps 5–6). Step 7 (expansion and refinement), as noted above, is intertwined throughout the paper.

Variations on this rule of thumb are inevitable. Appropriate adjustments must be made if the passage presents peculiar problems in one area, if reflection is omitted or expanded, and so on. The division of space for shorter or longer papers may be calculated proportionately following these guidelines.

In addition to deciding how to allocate space in your exegesis paper, you will also need to decide how precisely to approach the research and writing task itself. The primary goal of this book is to explain and illustrate the various elements of the exegetical process. Much of this process involves significant time spent in reading, thinking, taking notes, and "playing with" the text—much like any other paper. Some hints about how to do that are offered throughout the book. Additionally, Appendix B, "Practical Guidelines for Writing a Research Exegesis Paper," presents a step-by-step outline of five phases in the preparation of such a paper. This appendix serves as a useful summary of the entire book.

Moving Forward

Chapters 3–9 of this book each introduce a particular element of exegesis. Theoretically, once one of these chapters is mastered, a reader could execute that aspect of the exegetical process on a desert island. Readers who learn the entire exegetical process qualify as desert-island exegetes. Some final hints on the process are offered in chapter 10. Chapter 11 deals with expanding and refining each particular element of the exegetical process by using other resources and tools. In other words, chapter 11 is for those who have returned to civilization from the desert island and once again have a library, fellow readers, or other resources at their disposal. At the end of the book are appendixes that contain supplemental summary information as well as two sample exegesis papers.

Now that we have briefly examined the task of exegesis, we are prepared to study each of the steps more carefully. Before we can do that, however, we must consider the text that is the focus of our exegesis, namely, the Bible itself. That is the subject of the next chapter.

We conclude this introductory chapter with a quote from a literary critic. We may substitute the words "exegete" and "exegesis" for "explicator" and "explication":

> An explicator is a tour guide or traveling companion. The goal is to help a reader see what is really present in the [text]. A good explication is a lens that brings the text into focus.[23]

★ Chapter Summary

- Exegesis, a word deriving from the Greek verb "to lead out," is the careful historical, literary, and theological analysis of a text.

- Exegesis is investigation, conversation, and art.

- There are three basic approaches to exegesis: synchronic, diachronic ("historical-critical"), and existential.

---

[23] Ryken, *Words of Delight*, 208.

- The method advocated in this book is eclectic and integrated but gives priority to the synchronic approach. It emphasizes the importance of contexts.

- The seven elements of exegesis, and the steps in writing an exegesis paper, are: (1) survey (preparation for reading or introduction); (2) contextual analysis (of the text's historical and literary contexts); (3) formal analysis (of the text's form, structure, and movement); (4) detailed analysis; (5) synthesis; (6) reflection; and (7) expansion and refinement of the exegesis.

- Wise exegetes prepare a careful initial exegesis of the text on their own before consulting the experts.

↖ Practical Hints

1. I have always found it beneficial and have often required students to photocopy biblical passages for exegesis in order to "play with the text" or "think on paper." This means placing the text on a sheet of paper, with wide margins, and marking it up—underlining key phrases, circling recurrent terms, drawing lines between items, recording observations in the margins, and noting questions to be pursued. If you have access to electronic versions of the original languages or translations, you can download and rearrange your text however you like.

2. Remember, as you begin the process of exegesis, that there is much that can be and has been said about the Bible, some insightful and helpful, some of dubious value or extraneous. At first, observe and record whatever comes to mind. As you move through the hermeneutical circle, or weave the various strands of the exegetical process together, you will begin to sift the wheat from the chaff and begin looking for what really expresses the careful reading of the text that you are doing. Eventually, you will do the same as you read and take notes on what other interpreters have said. In the end, if you write an exegesis paper, you will have to decide what is and is not worth including from both your own thoughts and those of others. You will want to ask yourself, "Of all that I could say about this text in this paper, what truly expresses and supports the overall interpretation of the text that is emerging and that I find compelling?"

3. When you begin writing an exegesis paper, do not attempt to execute methods that are beyond your ability. A

beginning student should not attempt to do, say, tradition criticism without the skills to do it, or to discuss the intricacies of Hebrew grammar and vocabulary on the basis of an interlinear Bible. Rather, play to your strengths. Develop and use the skills any careful reader needs to have: observing, questioning, making connections, recognizing patterns, and so on. These will take you a long way.

👁 For Further Insight and Practice

1. Attempt a close reading of an editorial in a newspaper. What is its topic? What prompted the editorial? How is it structured? What key words, images, and themes appear in it? What sources or authorities, if any, does it quote? What is its main point? Is it effective? How and why? How do you react to it? Does it make you want to think or act differently?

2. Review chapter 11, section 1, pp. 148–55, "Resources for Understanding the Task," and peruse at least one of the books listed.

CHAPTER TWO
The Text

"A real translation is in the main an interpretation."
—*James Moffatt, Bible translator (1870–1944)*

How is a text selected for exegesis?

Which translations and editions of the Bible are best for exegesis?

In the previous chapter we considered the task of exegesis generally. Before we examine the various elements or steps of the exegetical process more carefully, we must consider the biblical text that will be the subject of our exegesis. This chapter begins with a discussion of how to choose a passage for exegesis. There follows a brief note on the Bible in the original languages and "interlinear Bibles." Since many exegetes work with an English text, even if they know some Hebrew or Greek, the bulk of the chapter is a consideration of what makes a good translation for purposes of exegesis and an examination of several Bible translations. Also included is a discussion of editions of the Bible in English (study Bibles).[1]

---

[1] Readers who know the biblical languages or are anxious to move on to the exegetical method itself may wish to skip the excursus for now and proceed to chapter 3 after reading the opening section of this chapter.

Choosing a Biblical Text for Exegesis

One of the most difficult and important decisions exegetes make is which biblical passage will be the focus of any particular exegetical investigation. For some people, of course, there is no decision to be made. A professor may assign a particular text to a student, or a religious tradition may assign a text to a preacher (normally by means of a lectionary, or calendar of readings). Most exegetes, however, especially those writing exegesis papers, have some choice. Even Christian preachers whose churches assign texts via a lectionary must choose which of the assigned readings to use as the basis of their preaching and whether to attempt to connect the readings together.[2]

There is no agreed-upon, generic technical term for the text that is studied in the exegetical process. The term *pericope* (Greek for *section,* related to the verb "to cut") is generally restricted to a segment of narrative biblical literature. Some linguistically minded scholars have introduced the terms *discourse* and *discourse unit,* but these terms have not yet gained general acceptance. The terms *text* and *passage,* both sufficiently generic and widely used, are appropriate for most purposes, with the term *pericope* being appropriate for a narrative text from books like Kings, Chronicles, the gospels, and Acts.

It is wise for beginning students to choose a text that interests them, but they should probably avoid "swimming in the deep water," that is, jumping into an extraordinarily difficult or controversial text.[3] More experienced students may

---

[2] Those from churches that use or adapt the Revised Common Lectionary should note that the first (Old Testament) and third (gospel) readings for each Sunday are chosen for their (purported) thematic or other relationship to each other, while the second (generally the epistle) reading is completely independent of the other two, except on certain special days.

[3] I owe this very appropriate analogy to my student Bill Garrison.

wish to explore a text that either excites them or confuses them, angers them or moves them. It may be a passage that has deep personal or ecclesial meaning or one upon which a complex doctrine or particular practice is grounded. It may be a text that seems to capture, or to violate, the spirit of a particular biblical writer or religious community. It may be a text that offends the potential exegete, so that he or she rejects its perceived claims or perspective. The more difficult or controversial the text, however, the more important it is for exegetes to acknowledge their biases—to themselves and perhaps even to their readers—upon undertaking the exegesis.

In any case, exegetes should have a desire to live with their texts for some period of time. Students, in particular, should ask, "Is this a text in which I want to invest a significant amount of my time, energy, and self?" "Do I have an interest in what others have said about this text?" And, practically speaking, "Am I willing to stake a significant portion of my course grade on a project related to this text?"

An exegesis paper considers a passage that is a complete unit of manageable size. In general, the passage should not be a single phrase or verse, nor should it be a complete chapter, much less an entire biblical book. A good rule of thumb for exegesis papers is somewhere between five and twenty-five verses, depending on the length and depth of the paper, the expectations of the professor, the character of the passage to be examined, and the biblical book in which the passage is located. In a ten-to-fifteen-page exegesis paper, a passage of about eight to twelve verses allows for about a page of discussion (or a little less) per verse, after the other aspects of exegesis are addressed. It is possible, of course, to write a shorter paper on a longer passage or a much longer paper on a much shorter passage. Beginning exegetes should always consult with their instructors.

Equally important is the question of beginning and ending points. It must first be remembered that almost every text appears in the middle of a larger text, so that it is not really an entity unto itself. Nonetheless, one of the basic units of human thought and expression seems to be something like the paragraph or stanza. These units, as well as longer units of thought and expression consisting of paragraphs and stanzas linked together, often begin and end with markers that indicate a difference or shift from what precedes and follows.

Exegetes should learn to look for indications of the beginning and end of units of thought and expression in the Bible. They should choose texts that have a clear start and finish and that communicate a coherent sequence of thought or action. As one scholar puts it, a text for exegesis should be "at least relatively self-contained and intending a specific effect."[4] Sometimes the beginning and/or end of the unit will contain logical markers (such as "therefore") or chronological markers (such as "next"). Sometimes a unit can be identified by the way its subject matter is distinct from that of the surrounding text. One common indication of a self-contained unit is the presence of *inclusio,* in which a word, phrase, or theme found at the beginning of the unit is echoed at the end. Another indication of the presence of a self-contained unit is *chiasmus,*[5] in which thoughts are organized into an ABB'A' pattern, with the initial thoughts mirrored back throughout the entire second half of the text. Sometimes there is a centerpiece or fulcrum in the middle of this structure (ABCB'A').[6]

One of the most obvious errors to avoid is selecting a passage that begins or ends in the middle of a thought or dramatic moment. Often identifying units is a matter of judgment. Consulting the divisions of the text in a Bible or a commentary may be a helpful starting point. Exegetes should not be bound, however, by the decisions of previous editors and commentators, nor even by the presence of verse and chapter numbers, which are not part of the text itself. Scholars introduced these tools for identifying and locating texts, but

---

[4] Werner Stenger, *Introduction to New Testament Exegesis* (Grand Rapids: Eerdmans, 1993), 24.

[5] From the Greek letter *chi,* X.

[6] Further discussion of these sorts of text structures can be found in chapter 5.

in doing so they made some mistakes. For example, they divided the chapters in 1 Corinthians at 11:1, when 11:1 is clearly the conclusion to chapter 10. If every Bible and every commentary fail to see the integrity and unity that you perceive in a set of verses, your contribution to the conversation about that passage may consist in part in identifying its status as a unit—especially if that status can be plausibly argued and can be shown to be significant for understanding the text.

The Bible in Its Original Languages

If you can read the biblical text in its original language, you should obviously do as much of your exegetical work as possible with the Hebrew or Greek text. The main current Greek and Hebrew critical editions are listed in section 2 of chapter 11.

Preparing your own working translation of the original text, to the best of your ability, is also helpful. This working translation will be modified throughout the exegetical process. Translations can still help, of course, by indicating possible interpretations and by guiding you through any mazes of difficult grammar and vocabulary.

One popular middle-ground between an English translation and a Hebrew Bible or Greek Testament is the "interlinear Bible," in which a very wooden translation of each word is placed above or below the line of Hebrew or Greek text. For readers who have some familiarity with the original language and use this tool as a way to refresh their memories, it may have a useful function if used cautiously. However, a little bit of knowledge of Hebrew or Greek can be dangerous, and combining such knowledge with the peculiar English renderings found in an interlinear Bible can be disastrous. People who do not read the original languages with some degree of competence should stay clear of interlinear Bibles and rely on good translations and solid research for their exegesis.

It is generally known that we do not possess the actual originals of the Bible. What we do possess are manuscripts that are copies of copies (and so on), and these manuscripts do not fully agree with one another. However, for the most part we have more and better copies of the biblical texts than we do of other documents from antiquity.

The art and science of studying these manuscripts, as well as early translations of the Bible, is called *textual criticism.* One of the goals of this field of study is to determine the most likely reading of every word of the Bible from among the several textual variants in each case. The judgments of textual critics about these variants appear in critical editions of the Bible in its original languages, and a very small percentage of them may sometimes be found in the footnotes of English translations.

Beginning exegetes should be aware of these issues, for they will be discussed in more technical commentaries and other works, and they do sometimes affect meaning in very significant ways. For example, some manuscripts of John 1:18 refer to Jesus Christ as the "only-begotten son," while others read "the only begotten God," perhaps meaning "the only begotten one, who is God." Understanding how these differences may have arisen and how scholars argue about them is both fascinating and challenging. Some books about the topic are listed in section 2 of chapter 11. In general, beginning exegetes will need to rely on the judgment of textual critics and translators, and they should refrain from amateur textual criticism. However, more experienced exegetes should learn enough about textual criticism to understand and eventually to make their own text-critical decisions.

Bible Translations (Versions) and Editions (Study Bibles)

Not everyone has the luxury of mastering ancient languages before doing exegesis. For those who do not read (or remember!) biblical Hebrew, Greek, and Aramaic, their first tool should be a good translation of the Bible. An additional aid is a scholarly, annotated edition of the Bible, or "study Bible." Many beginning exegetes do not understand why a professor recommends one translation or edition of the Bible and criticizes another, so this section attempts to explain the challenges of producing a good Bible translation and edition, and to comment on some of those available.

TRANSLATIONS

A Bible translation, or version, is a scholarly attempt to render the stories and thoughts of people from ancient cultures who spoke ancient languages into a modern language that is spoken by people who live in very different, contemporary cultures. Translation, like exegesis, is an art rather than a precise science. Every translation is itself an interpretation. Therefore, in a certain sense, every Bible translation is a kind of streamlined exegesis representing innumerable interpretive judgments and decisions. The artistic, interpretive character of translations is due to several factors—most of which we encounter when considering the elements of exegesis.

The first factor is the words themselves, *the lexical items,* and how they are combined, *the syntax.* Some words have a very limited range of functions or meanings in a language, but most words have a wide range of meaning. Furthermore, the function of many words changes when they are combined in phrases with other words or when used to serve particular rhetorical functions.

For example, the word *house* has quite different meanings in the following instances: "my friend's house"; "house of ill repute"; "house of David"; and "greenhouse." Similarly, the word *god* functions differently in each of the following phrases: "O my God, I am heartily sorry for having offended thee"; "Oh my God! What a beautiful dress!"; and "the god of this age." Even a simple phrase like "the love of God" is tricky: does it refer to *human* love for *God* or *God's* love for *us?* In the case of 1 John, one's rendering of this phrase is affected by, and will affect, one's interpretation of the document as a whole. As we will see in more detail in chapter 6, a word or phrase has a range of possible meanings; context narrows that range.

Further complicating the situation is the fact that the meaning of some words from ancient languages remains obscure, and the odd combination of words into idiomatic phrases (such as "pull the wool over my eyes") can turn individually clear lexical items into completely obscure phrases. The meaning of such words and phrases can sometimes only be guessed, using the context as a guide. In other words, meaning is not static; it is dynamic and dependent on context.

The second factor, therefore, is context—literary and rhetorical as well as historical, social, and cultural. The meaning of individual words, not to mention all the combinations of lexical items, depends on the greater literary context and rhetorical goals of the writing. Different writers use words differently, and the same writer may use the same word in different ways for different purposes. Moreover, the lexical items used by these writers point to historical, social, and cultural realities outside the text itself—extratextual items—that must be noticed and understood.

A third factor is the limitation inherent in all translation. The "target" language may not have a word or phrase to render accurately the meaning of a word or phrase in the "source" language. Even if appropriate lexical items exist in the target language, the resulting combination of words may be awkward, even to the point of being misleading. Good Hebrew syntax may yield horrible English syntax, and a good, literal English rendering may destroy the poetry or other artistic form and beauty of a Hebrew text. Furthermore, the target languages themselves evolve; for instance, the English spoken in the United States today differs markedly from that spoken in seventeenth-century England. Add to all of this the fact that frequently the translator and/or potential readers of the translation have no comparable cultural phenomenon to something mentioned or described in the text. For instance, how would one render the word *snow* for people who have never experienced it in person or via the media?

A "GOOD" TRANSLATION FOR EXEGESIS

Translators, it should be evident by now, have a daunting task. Good Bible translating demands a thorough knowledge of ancient languages and cultures as well as a sophisticated understanding of how best to bridge the linguistic and cultural gaps between then and now. It follows, therefore, that a translation produced by a team of reputable scholars drawing on years of study and research will be far superior to one produced by an individual or by a less qualified team.

What is unclear, however, is what the end-product created by such a scholarly team should look like. This lack of clarity is due to philosophical differences about the nature and purpose of translation. With respect to translations, scholars have sometimes distinguished between *word-for-word* or *literal* translations, on the one hand, and *idea-for-idea* or *dynamic-equivalence* translations, on the other. We can imagine a spectrum ranging from very literal to very dynamic, with every translation placed somewhere along the spectrum. Ordinary Bible readers sometimes distinguish between a translation and a paraphrase, the latter being understood as a less exact retelling that aims at rendering the general intent of a text in very understandable English (or another target language).

In recent decades, however, linguists have suggested that even what is often called a paraphrase should be called a translation, in part because all translation is interpretation. (A word-for-word translation of parts of any texts would, in fact, be a *mis*translation.) Linguists now prefer the terms *formal equivalence* and *functional equivalence* to literal and dynamic equivalence for defining the spectrum. Formal-equivalence translations emphasize the similarity in the linguistic forms (such as vocabulary and grammatical structures) between the source language and the target language. Functional-equivalence translations, on the other hand, stress the similarity in linguistic function (meaning) between the two languages.[7] Proponents of functional-equivalence

---

[7] An example of the difference between these two kinds of translations may be seen in the case of the French phrase "au revoir." A formal-equivalence approach to translation might stress the "literal" meaning of the words ("until the [time of] seeing [each other] again") and render it " 'til next time." A functional-equivalence approach would simply render the phrase "bye" or "see ya," depending on the context.

translations often claim that the goal of translation is to allow the translated text to have the same effect on contemporary readers that it did on ancient ones. (This goal is, however, both theoretically and pragmatically problematic.) For our purposes, we will define as a translation any English rendering of the Bible that is based on the original Hebrew, Greek, and Aramaic texts, no matter how functionally equivalent or even paraphrastic it may be.

Bible translators obviously approach the issue of formal versus functional translation theory differently, thereby yielding different kinds of translations. For instance, the principle of the translators of the New Revised Standard Version (NRSV) is "as literal as possible, as free as necessary." That represents a commitment to a largely formal-equivalence translation. On the other hand, the goal of the New Living Translation, which is the scholarly heir to the very popular Living Bible, was to produce a functional-equivalence, thought-for-thought translation that is accurate in both meaning and style.

No translation is perfect, and different kinds of translations fulfill different roles. For purposes of exegesis based on the English text of the Bible (as opposed to the original languages), a translation based on the theory of formal equivalence is best for two main reasons: (1) it allows more of the original ambiguities in the text to stand, and thus to be noticed, investigated, and interpreted by the exegete; and (2) it generally renders a recurring key word in the original biblical text with the same English word in the translation. Formal-equivalence translations are sometimes guilty, however, of creating odd, wooden renderings that do not sound much like English and that may even misinterpret the original text by giving precedence to form over function (meaning). But functional-equivalence translations, on the other hand, frequently (1) oversimplify complex or ambiguous texts and (2) substitute contemporary idiom for ancient biblical idiom, often resulting in inconsistent or misleading translations of key items. No matter how skillful the translators, the effect of these strategies on the exegete is prejudicial: one interpretation is given preference over another. This may be fine for the casual reader, but not for the serious exegete.

One possible strategy for addressing this problem is to use more than one translation. Reading several translations can indeed provide useful insights, but this approach is somewhat overrated and can lead to erroneous conclusions. Each translation still represents exegetical judgments, and the similarities and differences should not be given undue weight. Careful users of various translations should view the differences not as equally valid options but as *possible renderings* of the text, each of which has strengths and weaknesses that must be analyzed. In other words, translations suggest some (and not necessarily all) of a range of possible interpretations of particular texts. Only careful exegetical work will enable the reader to judge the various options. The notion that one translation is preferable to another because, on the surface, it is "easier to understand" or seems to "make more sense" is a mistaken one.

CHOOSING AN ENGLISH TRANSLATION FOR USE IN EXEGESIS

The following discussion evaluates the strengths and weaknesses of popular translations for purposes of exegesis. This evaluation is based on the criteria noted above: underlying translation theory; qualifications of the translator(s), including knowledge of biblical languages and contexts; and readability of the final result for readers of contemporary English. Only versions that contain, or are scheduled to contain, both Testaments are discussed. Most contemporary commentaries are based on or keyed to one or more of these translations.

Versions Preferred for Exegesis

The **Revised Standard Version** (RSV) was issued in stages from 1946 to 1977.[8] It continued the tradition of the King James Version (KJV) and its late-nineteenth-century revisions. The ongoing, first-rate translation committee, which was

---

[8] New Testament, 1946; Old Testament, 1952; Apocryphal/ Deuterocanonical books, 1957; revised New Testament, 1971; three additional texts canonical in the Eastern Orthodox churches, 1977.

ecumenical in composition, assured wide acceptance of the
final form of the RSV by all major Christian communions.
The RSV translators worked with a formal-equivalence approach to translation, in an age when functional equivalence was not a serious option. The result was an excellent
formal-equivalence (self-styled "literal") translation informed
by the best scholarship of the day and based on the best
critical editions of the text available. The RSV has been sup-
planted by the NRSV (see below), but it is still very useful as
the basis for exegesis of the English text.

The **New American Bible** (NAB) is, in the United States, the
standard translation by and for Roman Catholics. It contains, therefore, the deuterocanonical books. Produced by a
team of superior Roman Catholic biblical scholars, it first
appeared in 1970. The New Testament was revised in 1986
and the Psalms in 1991, in consultation with non-Catholic
scholars; a fully revised Old Testament is still underway.
The NAB translators deliberately chose to reject a functional-equivalence approach and to follow a policy of formal equivalence, placing their work in the tradition of the
RSV. Two of their stated reasons for this decision were to
promote deeper study of the Bible and to avoid subjectivity
(perhaps idiosyncrasy would be the better word) in the
translation. Although the NAB is a foreign book to many
non-Catholics and its diction and choice of vocabulary often
outside the mainstream of better-known biblical translations like the KJV and RSV/NRSV, it is generally a very good
translation. It could be the textual basis for exegesis, but
probably in tandem with the RSV or NRSV.

The **New Revised Standard Version** (NRSV), completed
in 1989, is the successor to the RSV and follows a formal-
equivalence principle that its translators identify in the words
"as literal as possible, as free as necessary." The committee
of superior scholar-translators, chaired by Bruce Metzger,
made several major stylistic changes to the RSV. One was the
elimination of archaic pronoun and verb forms (thou, thee,
thine; art, hast, etc.). Another, more significant change was the
introduction of gender-inclusive language for human beings
whenever the pronouns or addressees implied either both

men and women or any person, without reference to gender. This was accomplished, for example, by pluralizing singular male pronouns to "they"/"them"; replacing "brothers" with "brothers and sisters"; and substituting "mortal(s)" for "man"/"men." This was a minor concession to the principle of dynamic equivalence. Occasionally, however, the result is exegetically problematic, for example, when Paul's use of the word "brother(s)" is replaced, not by "brothers and sisters," but by "believer(s)" or "friend(s)."

The resulting translation, based on the best available critical editions of both Testaments (including the apocryphal/deuterocanonical books) and, for the most part, respecting the principle of formal equivalence, is excellent as a basis for English-language exegesis. It is not a perfect translation, of course, but it is by most accounts the best now available in English, especially for in-depth study.

Versions Acceptable for Exegesis, with Caution

The **New American Standard Bible** (NASB) was published by the conservative evangelical Lockman Foundation in 1971, with an update in 1995 (sometimes abbreviated as NAS95). The update improves the version's readability in many ways, most obviously in the elimination of out-of-date vocabulary, including "thees" and "thous." It is the Bible of choice in certain circles and completely unknown in others. The NASB/NAS95 is a formal-equivalence translation in the KJV-ASV (American Standard Version) tradition that is sometimes characterized as possessing a "wooden literalism." The publisher claims that this "word-for-word" translation is the "most literal" in English and that "[a]t NO point did the translators attempt to interpret Scripture through translation."[9] Thus they claim to convey the Word of God better than any other English translation.

However, all translation is interpretation, and the NASB update continues the KJV tradition of supplying italicized

---

[9] See the following page on the Lockman foundation website: http://www.gospelcom.net/lockman/trans/nasbov.htm.

English words for missing words in the Hebrew and Greek original. All translations must "fill in the blanks," so to speak (though italicizing the additions is no longer the norm), but to do so is clearly an act of interpretation. Thus the NASB/NAS95 is not as "literal" as it claims. Moreover, its translation team is not of the same scholarly caliber as the NIV or NRSV. All in all, the NASB update is generally an acceptable formal-equivalence translation.

The **Revised English Bible** (REB) is the 1989 revision of the disastrous New English Bible (NEB) from the 1960s and early 1970s. Its style is vivid British, and it frequently provides compelling reading by means of its turns of language while avoiding the excesses of its predecessor. Linguistically, it walks a kind of middle ground between formal and functional equivalence. Though it could be used in an emergency for exegesis, it is best used, not as the main basis for exegesis, but as a significant second translation and a source for well-worded interpretations of standard exegetical decisions.

The **New International Version** (NIV), released by the International Bible Society in 1973 (NT) and 1978 (full Bible), was intended in part, like the NASB, to be an evangelical Protestant alternative to the RSV for those dissatisfied with the KJV. Its team of translators was quite good, using the standard critical editions of the text rather than the texts that were the basis of the KJV. A team of reviewers for readability aided the process of translation. The NIV is a combination of formal and functional equivalence in its approach. The preface to the NIV says that the translators' "first concern" was the "accuracy of the translation and its fidelity to the thought of the biblical writers" and that they have "striven for more than a word-for-word translation" in order to accomplish "faithful communication of the meaning of the writers of the Bible." They do this by means of "frequent modifications in sentence structure and constant regard for the contextual meaning of words."

Occasionally the theological perspective of the translators (or perhaps reviewers and editors) colors the translation a bit too boldly (a kind of functional-equivalence theory at work), but in general the NIV captures the substance and/or the spirit of the text well. With some notable exceptions, however, its renderings do not match the quality of the RSV-NRSV tradition. Moreover, its modifications of syntax and attention to context introduce a higher degree of interpretation into the translation than do the RSV and NRSV. There are currently discussions taking place at the publisher about a new NIV with more gender-inclusive language in referring to human beings.

Versions Unacceptable as the Basis for Exegesis, but Useful in Other Ways

The following versions, though unacceptable as the basis for exegesis, have specific merits that can assist in the interpretive process, and some of these are noted.

The Message, a complete New Testament, was published by NavPress in 1993. It is the fruit of an ongoing translation project of the Reverend Eugene Peterson, a Presbyterian pastor with a significant degree of scholarly acumen (resulting, in part, from graduate studies at the Johns Hopkins University). Peterson's laudable goal is pastoral—to render the biblical text into contemporary idiom, operating with a clear theory of functional equivalence. The result is an exegesis, but it is not itself the basis for exegesis. Like the work of an earlier scholar-pastor, the British self-styled "paraphraser" J. B. Phillips, *The Message* is probably best used to help express in contemporary idiom the exegetical judgments that an exegete makes on the basis of work on the original texts or other English translations, and through research. Some of Peterson's idiomatic renderings, however, are rather odd.

The **Good News Bible** (GNB) was produced by the American Bible Society, beginning with the New Testament (Today's English Version) in 1966 and the full Bible in 1971. The translators, who were quite sophisticated in their knowledge of the Bible and linguistics, employed a theory of functional equivalence and geared their translation to persons with a somewhat limited vocabulary. Its strengths for its intended audience, however, are its weaknesses for exegesis. It should be consulted, if at all, only as one possible rendering, both exegetically and stylistically, of the text. It should not be the sole basis for serious study.

The **Contemporary English Version** (CEV) appeared in 1995, also published by the American Bible Society from the perspective of functional equivalence. The CEV attempts especially to interpret sensitive biblical texts more appropriately and accurately, especially New Testament references to Jews. The translators argue that terms like "the Jews" are better rendered, depending on the context, by phrases like "the religious leaders" or "the people." The principle itself, as well as its application, causes problems for those doing exegesis, since it makes some very significant and debatable exegetical judgments. As in the case of the GNB, so also with the CEV: it may be consulted as one possible rendering of the text, both exegetically and stylistically, but it should not be used as the basis for exegesis. Of these two translations, the CEV is perhaps the better.

The **New Living Translation** (NLT) is a bold, vast improvement over the Living Bible (see below), and it was issued in 1996 by the same evangelical publisher, Tyndale House. The NLT was produced by a team of excellent biblical scholars using the best available critical editions of the original languages and guided by an explicit principle of functional equivalence. The translators were especially sensitive to cultural context, attempting to render lexical items referring to means of measuring (weight, distance, time, monetary worth, etc.) and to everyday customs and realities of life into parallel English idioms. (The NLT, for example, puts the contemporary equivalent of measurements and the like in the text and the original words in a footnote, while formal-equivalence translations generally do just the opposite.) The result for exegesis, however, even if one agrees with the translators' functional equivalents, is that too many exegetical judgments have been made and too many cultural customs interpreted. Thus the NLT can and should be used as an interpretation, and usually a very insightful one, but not as the basis for exegesis.

The **New Jerusalem Bible** (NJB, 1985) is the complete revision of the 1966 Jerusalem Bible (JB), an English translation of a French translation of the original languages. The French tended toward the functional end of the translation spectrum, and the English JB followed suit. As a translation of a translation, and a relatively nonformal one at that, the JB should never have served as the basis of exegetical work. The NJB translators worked directly from the original languages, but the product still tends toward the functional end of the spectrum. It is therefore a useful tool for exploring and expressing exegetical options, but it should not serve as the basis for exegesis.

Versions Unacceptable for Exegesis

The **Living Bible** (LB), produced in the 1960s and published in 1971, is a paraphrase of the King James Version and is not based on the original languages. It reflects the theological perspective and lack of scholarly biblical training of its producer, Kenneth Taylor. While this paraphrase has made the Bible accessible to many, it possesses no scholarly value. Its successor, the **New Living Translation**, is discussed above.

The **King James Version** (KJV), or **Authorized Version** (AV), was produced in 1611 by a team of translators. They generally followed an implicit theory of formal equivalence, but, unfortunately, they worked with generally late and less reliable biblical manuscripts. Since 1611, many older and better manuscripts of the Bible have been discovered, and modern research in the area of textual criticism (which includes comparing and contrasting manuscripts to produce a "critical edition" of the original text) has given us a different basis of original texts to translate than that used by the KJV translators. This means that an exegesis using the KJV may sometimes be analyzing one or more words, phrases, or verses that did not actually appear in the original biblical text.

In addition, biblical scholarship and linguistics have both progressed significantly during the last four hundred years, providing countless pieces of data and perspectives for translating the text more accurately. Moreover, the English language has changed enormously in the same four-hundred-year period, rendering much of the KJV's language obsolete.

Taken together, these factors mean that the King James Version is completely unacceptable as the basis for serious, scholarly study of the Bible. The **New King James Version** (NKJV), released in 1979 (NT) and 1982 (OT), updates obsolete language and attempts to be a more linguistically sophisticated translation than the KJV. However, because it is based on the same problematic manuscript tradition, it too is unacceptable for exegesis.

To summarize the preceding discussion, we may list these versions in four categories: (1) those that are the best as the basis for exegesis (RSV, NAB, NRSV); (2) those that can serve as the basis for exegesis, if used with caution (NAS95, REB, NIV); (3) those that provide helpful exegetical or stylistic renderings but should not serve as the basis for exegesis (*The Message*, GNB, CEV, NLT, NJB); and (4) those unacceptable as the basis of exegesis (LB, KJV/AV, NKJV).

Preferred for Exegesis	Acceptable for Exegesis, with Caution	Unacceptable for Exegesis, but Helpful in Other Ways	Unacceptable for Exegesis
RSV	NAS95	*The Message*	LB
NAB	REB	GNB	KJV (AV)
NRSV	NIV	CEV	NKJV
		NLT	
		NJB	

Of all these translations, the NRSV is probably the overall best to use for exegesis, but even this can be usefully compared with other translations.

One helpful publication, *The Complete Parallel Bible* (New York and Oxford: Oxford University Press, 1993), presents four major translations in parallel columns (NRSV, REB, NJB, NAB). This format will often alert the reader to major translational/exegetical options in the text.

EDITIONS (STUDY BIBLES)

Most publishers that are licensed to publish the various translations of the Scriptures issue a variety of editions of the Bible. Some are "plain-vanilla" editions, containing only the notes that are provided by the translators. Others add section headings, cross-references to other biblical texts, pronunciation guides, abbreviated concordances (lists of key words and their biblical references), glossaries, and other helps for readers. There are still others, which we will call "study Bibles," that provide some or all of the afore-mentioned helps as well as introductions to each book of the Bible. They also include footnotes explaining the gist of stories and arguments, illuminating historical and cultural references, presenting translational and exegetical options and difficulties, listing relevant cross-references, and offering brief interpretive commentary. Some even provide general articles on the Bible and biblical study and questions for study and reflection.

These study Bibles are, however, of uneven quality—even more so than the translations with which they are associated. Some are produced by well-meaning but academically unqualified people and publishing houses. Others are "spiritually" or "devotionally" oriented, which is a worthy enterprise, but which should not be mistaken for encouraging scholarly exegesis.

The great value of a sound, scholarly study Bible is that it provides quick, reliable (though not infallible!), "context-sensitive" help. Every serious student of the Bible should use one on a regular basis. For purposes of exegesis, of course, a study Bible does not provide enough detail, but it can be suggestive for a variety of exegetical matters (especially context, structure, and synthesis). It also allows readers to peruse a particular portion of a biblical book, an entire book, or a series of books with some degree of comfort, in much the same way as they might use an annotated road map from one of the travel clubs. Finally, it normally provides readers with a very helpful array of cross-references at a glance, leading them to important parallel texts and possible sources in earlier writings.

There are four particularly helpful scholarly study Bibles from which to choose. Many of these appear in several forms (paperback, hardcover, "student," electronic, etc.)

for a variety of prices, but all have an excellent cost-to-value ratio.

The New Oxford Annotated Bible (with the Apocrypha; New York: Oxford University Press, 1991; 3d ed., forthcoming) of the NRSV translation is the successor to the same title produced for the RSV, which combined *The Oxford Annotated Bible* and *The Oxford Annotated Apocrypha*. With the publication of the NRSV, the annotations and articles were reviewed and updated by an ecumenical team of superb scholars. The introductions to each book are generally brief (a page or less) but insightful. The notes, printed a bit smaller than the text, are also often brief (averaging 10 to 20 percent of the page), though in some documents, particularly in the New Testament, they consume an average of one-third of the page.

The greatest strengths of this study Bible are probably the other helps it offers, particularly the introductions to the various sections of the Bible (Pentateuch, prophetic books, apocalyptic literature, etc.), as well as general articles on such topics as "Characteristics of Hebrew Poetry" and "Literary Forms in the Gospels." Some charts and maps round out the volume.

All in all, this is a good study Bible. Its quality is first-rate, but its brevity makes it less desirable than some others.

The NIV Study Bible (Grand Rapids: Zondervan, 1985, 1995) was produced at the initiative of some of the original NIV translators. The copious notes (frequently 50 percent of the page, and set in smaller, different type) unabashedly reflect the "traditional evangelical theology" of the contributors. One major theme of the notes is the "interrelationship of the Scriptures," a legitimate concern that sometimes results in the drawing of parallels and theological conclusions that some may consider questionable, especially in notes on Old Testament texts that are seen as pointing ahead to the New.

In addition to the notes, *The NIV Study Bible* has introductions to each book (most of which reflect "traditional" views of authorship and date, such as Mosaic authorship of the

Pentateuch) with detailed outlines; a cross-reference system for texts and themes; dozens of maps and charts related to various books; a few brief essays; indexes; and a very substantial concordance.

This study Bible's great strengths are its helpful charts and notes, plus its inclusion of a concordance. Unfortunately, however, the introductions are defensive (of "traditional" perspectives) in tone and the notes occasionally too biased in one theological direction. Used with awareness of the theological perspective and agenda of the contributors, this study Bible can be useful for providing a general survey, but its judgments need balance for serious academic study.

The HarperCollins Study Bible (New York: HarperCollins, 1993) of the NRSV was produced for the publisher by members of the Society of Biblical Literature, the world's largest and foremost association of professional biblical scholars. The introductions (generally 2–3 pages) and notes (generally 35 to 40 percent of the page, but sometimes 50 percent, set in type slightly smaller than the text) reflect a range of contemporary scholarly opinion from a wide variety of religious traditions. This study Bible does not have any general articles, apart from a brief introduction, but it does contain some helpful charts and more than twenty-five maps. Although the annotations are very responsible and reliable, they tend to focus only on historical and literary matters, to the neglect of theological concerns.

The Catholic Study Bible (New York: Oxford University Press, 1990) is a textbook, even a library, in one volume. Although produced exclusively by Roman Catholic scholars, it is not theologically biased and can be used with great profit by any student. Each introduction to a biblical book (generally 1–2 pages) is supplemented at the front of the volume by a "Reading Guide" to the book. The reading guides, which are all excellent, provide much longer introductions to each book's author, historical and social context, structure, content, theology, and spiritual significance. Each reading guide concludes with a short bibliography. The brief introductions and reading guides are further supplemented by general articles about biblical study, each of the major divisions of the Bible, and biblical archaeology and geography. In addition to maps, the back of the volume has lectionary tables, indicating which texts are read on which days throughout each of the three years of the Roman Catholic Church's liturgical schedule.

The notes in *The Catholic Study Bible* are printed in small type and take up anywhere from about 10 to 60 percent of the page, with an average of less than 20 percent for the Old Testament but 35 to 40 percent for the New Testament. These notes emphasize careful analysis of the structure and theology of the text, with copious cross-references. All in all, this is the best study Bible on the market. Its notes are balanced and insightful, while its reading guides put the detailed comments into larger historical, literary, and theological perspectives.

In the end, then, unfortunately, the best *study* Bible (*The Catholic Study Bible*) does not contain the best American English translation for exegetical purposes (the NRSV). Students must therefore decide on the translation that best suits their purposes and then pick the best study Bible to match it—or vice versa.

★ Chapter Summary

- Students should select a passage for exegesis that interests them and that is a complete unit of manageable size with a clear beginning and end.

- Every translation is an interpretation, a kind of streamlined exegesis.

- The task of translation is rendered difficult by several complicating features of language.

- The two basic approaches to translation are formal equivalence and functional equivalence.

- Students who do not read the original languages should use a formal-equivalence translation such as the NRSV, NAB, or RSV as the basis of their exegetical work.

- Study Bibles are a valuable tool, though none is without its limitations.

⌐ Practical Hints

1. Treat all translations, even the best, as carefully researched options, not as the final truth.

2. If you do not read the original languages, use a formal translation such as the NRSV or NAB as the basis of your exegesis, and use other versions to supply possible translations or interpretations of various elements—any and all of which must be confirmed by careful exegesis.

3. Purchase a good study Bible for everyday use and for basic helps in the beginning stages of exegesis.

◉ For Further Insight and Practice

1. Choose two favorite Bible texts and read them in at least three different translations. What differences do you notice? Are the differences significant? Does the tone or thrust of either passage differ, in your estimation, from translation to translation?

2. Compare the treatment of these two passages in two different study Bibles, and record your observations about the differences in interpretation.

3. Review chapter 11, section 2, pp. 155–60, "Resources for Understanding the Text."

CHAPTER THREE

Survey

THE FIRST ELEMENT

> "Think of yourself as a detective looking for clues
> to a [text's] general theme or idea, alert for
> anything that will make it clearer."
> —*Mortimer J. Adler and Charles Van Doren*,
> How to Read a Book[1]

On first reading, what seems to be going on in the text?

The careful reading and analysis of any text, whether textbook, essay, or poem, requires an initial survey of the contents of the document. Such a survey prepares the reader, alerting him or her to key aspects of the text for consideration in the process of closer reading. So too when reading the Bible. This very short (but very important) chapter introduces some simple strategies for surveying the passage to be studied in its context. Important tools for assisting in this part of the exegetical process are discussed in section 3 of chapter 11.

Survey and Question

When I was in elementary school, our teacher taught us a reading skill—actually a process—for "attacking" a chapter

---

[1] Mortimer J. Adler and Charles Van Doren, *How to Read a Book* (rev. ed.; New York: Simon & Schuster, 1972), 36.

in a textbook. It was abbreviated SQ3R. The letters stood for *survey, question, read, recite,* and *review.* The starting point for SQ3R is obviously "survey": getting the lay of the land, so to speak. It is an initial overview of the contents of your chosen text in context.

In a similar way, today we have learned to navigate the electronic equivalent of a chapter, the website, by surveying its contents before plunging into the many layers of the site. A glance at the home page, with its navigation bars and clickable links, provides a bird's-eye view of the major components of the site.

Unlike textbooks or essays in newspapers and magazines, the Bible (apart from the Psalms) has no original chapter titles, headlines, or subheads to indicate the specific contents of a chapter or section—and certainly no navigation bars! The section titles found in many Bibles are the work—sometimes good, sometimes not so good—of the editors of each particular version or edition. Thus the first step in interpretation is to read the passage several times, ignoring the section titles—or at least recognizing that they are the work of other readers. You may even wish to give the passage your own preliminary title.

Many people find it beneficial to read the text in a few different translations (as well as in Greek or Hebrew, if you are able). It may also be helpful to read the text aloud, recalling that much biblical literature was actually heard before it was ever read. Furthermore, it is important to read the text within its context, to read (or at the very least, skim) the book or a major section of the book in which the text is found.

As you read, you should begin to record observations and questions that come to mind. These notes may be about the place of the text in the biblical book, the historical and social situation of the writer or audience, allusions to texts or other items in the passage, the form and contents of the selection, and so on. This is the "question" step of the SQ3R process.

It is also helpful at this early point to read a brief introduction to the biblical book in which the passage is located, especially if you are reading it "cold"—that is, apart from the context of class discussion or reading assignments. Some study editions of the Bible provide such good introductions. Other good sources would be a short article in an introductory textbook, a Bible dictionary, or a one-volume commentary. (These are discussed in section 3 of chapter 11.) Reading these items will likely raise additional questions that you will want to investigate as your exegesis progresses.

Do *not*, however, read much commentary on the text itself at this point in the exegetical process. Do your own work first! You may wish, nevertheless, to use the one-volume commentary or a similar resource to get a basic grasp of the themes and issues in the interpretation of your text before you proceed to more in-depth reading.

Exegetes who read the original languages should also make a provisional translation of the text at this stage. The translation process itself will raise all kinds of issues for the exegetical investigation.

First Impressions: Educated Guessing

As you execute and complete your first readings of the text and its contexts, you will begin to formulate some initial impressions of its meaning. Ask yourself, "What is the topic of this text? What perspective on the topic does it offer? What role might it play in the book as a whole?" At this point, answering such questions is often little more than educated guesswork—but it is an important first step in the process of exegesis. The great theorist of interpretation Paul Ricoeur says that there are no rules for guessing. However, the surveying and guessing process will lead you to continue with a more systematic investigation as you move on to the remaining steps of the process.

Furthermore, though there may be no hard-and-fast rules for guessing, Ricoeur also reminds us that this early encounter with the text in context provides a good opportunity for readers to acknowledge any prior understanding of—or bias about—the text. Do you know this text? Have you heard or read it before? Does its topic or perspective stir up any memories or feelings, whether positive or negative? It is also an opportunity to examine your own socio-theological location—your own social status, gender, culture, and religious beliefs—to see how they may affect your initial and ongoing encounter with the text.

The process of "educated guessing" should result in your formulation of a working thesis about the meaning of the text. This working thesis will be constantly revised and reformulated as your exegetical work continues. In fact, your final interpretation of a text may be quite contrary to your preliminary educated guess.

Writing an Introduction

In an exegesis paper, as in any paper, the first part should be a brief statement of the contents and thesis, or main point, of the paper. Your thesis statement, begun as an educated guess, will be honed and refined throughout the exegetical process. By the time you finalize your thesis statement for the introduction, it should be more than a guess. Although any biblical interpretation should be held with humility and an appropriate degree of tentativeness, a good paper presents a clear thesis and argues it vigorously.

The opening of the paper may contain highlights from one or more of the main sections of the paper, especially the sections on context and synthesis. For this reason, of course, the introduction will be written after the process of interpretation is completed. Some exegetes today also feel the need to identify their socio-theological location in the introduction to a paper or longer work. Although this is unobjectionable in principle, if handled carefully, the introduction to a paper is not the place for an extended self-description or confession.

★ Chapter Summary

- The process of initially surveying and questioning the text in context gives the reader the "lay of the land" and allows for the formulation of observations and questions to investigate.

- The initial survey includes taking an educated guess at the text's meaning.

- The introduction to an exegesis paper, finalized at the conclusion of the exegetical process, presents the thesis of the paper in light of the results of the exegetical process.

↰ Practical Hints

1. Begin recording thoughts and questions from your very first encounter with the text.

2. Remember that guessing is not a bad reading strategy—as long as you remember to allow your first impressions to be refined, expanded, and corrected.

◉ For Further Insight and Practice

1. Using a Bible with section or chapter titles, read the following well-known passages, noting the title supplied by the editors and writing one of your own.

Passage	Editor's Title	Your Title
Genesis 1:1–2:3		
Exodus 12:31–42		
Luke 15:11–32		
John 3:1–21		

2. Review chapter 11, section 3, pp. 160–65, "Resources for Surveying the Text."

3. Choose a one-volume commentary and learn as much as you can about the book of Isaiah and the basic contents of Isaiah 40–55 (chs. 40–55) in fifteen minutes. Then look at Isaiah 40:1–11 and make an initial guess at the gist of its message.

4. Read carefully the introductions to the sample exegesis papers at the end of this book, Appendixes C and D.

CHAPTER FOUR

Contextual Analysis

THE SECOND ELEMENT

The Historical and Literary Contexts of the Text

"A text without a context is a pretext."
—*Anonymous*

"The devil can cite Scripture for his purpose."
—*William Shakespeare*, The Merchant of Venice
I, iii, 99

Oh that I knew how all thy lights combine,
And the configurations of their glorie!
Seeing not onely how each verse doth shine,
But all the constellations of the storie!
—*George Herbert*, "The Holy Scriptures (II)"

In what historical, social, and cultural situation was the passage written?

How does the passage relate to what precedes and follows it, and to the document as a whole?

The Bible did not just "drop out of heaven," nor was it written in a special language with unique literary forms by some strange class of humans unaffected by their social and historical situation. No, the Bible was written by and for real people, living in specific historical contexts, to address particular individual and community needs. (This does *not* necessarily imply, however, that the Bible is *merely* a human book. Jews and Christians have always believed that the

Bible was the result of some combination of human and divine effort.) Close analysis of a biblical text requires careful attention to its historical and literary contexts.

Indeed, context is so crucial to interpretation that it is no exaggeration whatsoever to say that if you alter the *context* of a word or sentence or paragraph, you also alter the *content* of that text. Sometimes the effect is relatively minimal, but often it can be very significant. For example, the meaning of a person shouting "Fire!" will be very different depending upon the context: while running out of a house engulfed in flames, while sitting inside a movie theater that is not burning, or while standing beside a line of men armed with rifles facing a lone man who is blindfolded.

In this chapter we consider the historical (including social and cultural) and the literary (including rhetorical) contexts of a text.

Historical, Social, and Cultural Contexts

People and communities are constituted in large measure by

- the significant events they experience (either personally or vicariously through stories) and retell;
- the relationships in which they are engaged; and
- the values that they embrace, knowingly or not.

These facets of human life—our (1) historical, (2) social, and (3) cultural contexts—were also, of course, facets of life in "Bible times." Of all elements of exegesis, understanding the historical, social, and cultural contexts—which we will refer to as "historical context" for short—is the most difficult for the nonscholar (and even for the scholar!).[1] Reconstruct-

---

[1]There is no one ideal term to refer to the complex reality that is embodied in the long phrase "historical, social, and cultural contexts." To those who emphasize the socio-cultural dimension, "historical" is sometimes taken to refer only to events, with insufficient attention to cultural values and networks of social relationships. Because I find the term "social context" inadequate

ing the historical contexts of the biblical writings is a never-ending task in which professional biblical scholars, historians, and others are engaged. Because historical reconstruction is an arduous task, because it is in part art as well as science, and because it is always changing as new discoveries are made and new theories are advanced, some readers of the Bible conclude that the real-life context of the biblical writings can be ignored. Some would even argue that we imperil ourselves and our readings if we make interpretation dependent on historical, social, and cultural contexts.

The approach taken in this book is that the task of understanding the worlds of the Bible and of particular texts is necessary, albeit difficult. Texts are often the product of specific occasions, composed to address certain needs, and neglecting these contexts is more perilous than the risk of making mistakes in our historical reading. People communicate within a social network located within a particular culture at a specific point in time. Our goal, in part, is to discover the social network within which the writers and hearers/readers of biblical texts communicated. We also want to discover the common cultural beliefs and values—the "presupposition pool," as some have called it—that authors and hearers/readers of the original text would have brought to their production of and encounter with the text. Making this challenging process all the more complex is the fact that the sources, authors, and readers/hearers of the text may well have all had different social networks and presupposition pools!

The average reader cannot possibly know in detail the complex stories of ancient nations, communities of faith, and individuals that are the concern of biblical scholars and historians. Most people must rely on the technical works or more popular publications of these scholars. These can be found in books, Bible dictionaries, commentaries, scholarly journals, and certain magazines written by scholars for nonscholars. (Some of these works are listed in section 4 of

---

and the term "socio-rhetorical context" cumbersome, I have chosen to use the term "historical context," but I mean it in the broadest sense possible.

chapter 11.) Modern scholars draw on more traditional approaches to history and also on relatively new approaches that are indebted to such social sciences as sociology and cultural anthropology. Some are interested primarily in *social description,* or *what,* while others are interested in *social analysis,* or *why,* often by using standard models and procedures from the social sciences. The goal of all of these approaches is to understand the contexts of the biblical texts as thoroughly as possible—the social and political environment in which texts were written, the cultural values expressed in or challenged by the texts, and so on.

As you read a biblical text, questions about these sorts of topics will naturally arise. They should be noted carefully for investigation. Using one or more of the kinds of resources noted above, you should attempt to answer these questions as well as find out as much as you can about the historical, social, and cultural situation in which the author and readers lived:

- What were the chief characteristics of the people (often referred to as the "community") addressed by the passage? What can be known of their history? social location? beliefs and practices?

- What ancient events, customs, values, and beliefs are mentioned or alluded to in the text that must be understood in order to comprehend the text?

- What situation seems to have prompted the author to write this text?

Discerning the situation of the author and readers is often tricky business. Many times, for instance, exegetes assume that a word or phrase in a narrative text about Israel or Jesus is an allusion to a particular belief, situation, or problem in the later community to which the text was written. While the existence of such connections is plausible, even likely, the burden of proof is on the exegete to demonstrate specific connections. A related problem is sometimes called "mirror reading," the attempt to reconstruct the beliefs and practices of a community on the basis of what is said not only about them but also to them, especially in a New Testament letter. The careful exegete wants to make sure that such reconstructions do not constitute a house of cards on which one's exegesis is built.

Nevertheless, despite these words of caution, understanding as much as possible of the historical, social, and cultural contexts is absolutely essential to exegesis. For example, you cannot grasp either the irony or the message of the story of the "good Samaritan" (Luke 10:25–37) unless you understand something of first-century Jewish–Samaritan relations. Nor can you understand Ezekiel's vision of dry bones coming to life (Ezekiel 37) without some knowledge of Israel's spiritual and political destruction, exile to Babylon, and consequent despair.

Since you cannot, and should not, read (or write!) a lengthy history book relevant to your text, ask yourself what are the *key* facts and issues related to this passage (and the book in which it is found) that will help you interpret it. It is these key things that you must focus on in your research and, when you write an exegesis paper, point out to your reader. A hermeneutical circle will be at work: the more you learn about the context, the sharper your questions will become and the more able you will be to zero in on that which really matters.

Literary and Rhetorical Contexts

It has been said that a text without a context is a pretext—an excuse for finding one's presuppositions confirmed by the text. In other words, many misinterpretations of the Bible are due to neglect of the literary context. To understand a passage, you must try to see how it fits into the larger literary unit(s) in which it occurs: for instance, the chapter, section of the biblical book, and the book as a whole. Literary context, therefore, is really context*s*—plural. The text is often like the center of a set of concentric circles, each circle representing a larger section of the biblical book. These contexts are usually referred to as the *nearer,* or *immediate,* context and the *larger* context(s).

One helpful, almost necessary, tool in the task of contextual analysis is an outline, even a brief one, of the book of the

Bible in which the passage occurs. Outlines can be found in many editions of the Bible and in Bible dictionaries, introductory texts, and commentaries. Ideally, however, students should construct their own outlines of biblical books that they study.

In addition to the literary context, a text also has a *rhetorical* context. Rhetoric is the art of effective (and therefore often persuasive) speaking and writing. According to Cicero, the purpose of rhetoric is to teach, delight, and move hearers or readers. Rhetorical context, therefore, refers to the place of a passage in the document's overall strategy of rational, artistic, and/or emotional influence and persuasion. Rhetorical context is a function of literary context, but it is more. Analyzing the literary context means asking *where* a text is located; analyzing the rhetorical context means asking *why* a text is located where it is. The fundamental question is what *effect* the text has, or might have, on readers by virtue of its situation within a larger discourse.

The average exegete, and even the biblical scholar, cannot be expected to grasp all the intricacies of rhetorical criticism. Some of the basic structures of rhetoric indicated in the next chapter are helpful to know, but perhaps the single most important tool for rhetorical analysis is the disciplined imagination. Constantly ask yourself, as you look at the text, "Why *this* and why *here?* If I am the hearer/reader, what do I sense this text trying to 'do to me'?"

As you consider literary and rhetorical contexts, then, you will be asking yourself the following kinds of questions:

FOR THE LARGER CONTEXTS

- Where does this passage occur in the structure of the book, and what significance does this position have?
- What has "happened" (whether in narrative, argument, etc.) in the book so far?
- Of what major section is this unit a part?
- What appears to be its function in the section and in the book as a whole? How does this passage appear to serve the agenda of the entire work?

FOR THE IMMEDIATE CONTEXT

- What is the subject of the paragraph or two immediately preceding this passage? How does this material lead into the passage at hand?

- Does the material following the passage connect directly to it or help explain it?

- Does this passage work in connection with its immediate context to achieve a particular rhetorical goal?

It should be clear that the process of analyzing the literary context of a text entails hard work. It means reading more than the short passage you are trying to understand or analyze. But it is necessary hard work if you really want to grasp the meaning of a biblical text. (Thus, those who use a lectionary for preaching must be especially faithful in reading the passages for the week in a Bible, not just in the lectionary.) More often than not your subsequent detailed analysis of the text will cause you to modify your initial conclusions about the literary and rhetorical contexts—as you would probably have expected by now.

Conclusion

A text without a context—a text isolated from its various contexts (plural)—is a potentially dangerous weapon. Responsible exegesis acknowledges the difficulty of discovering those contexts, whether historical, social, cultural, literary, or rhetorical in nature, but refuses to abandon the task. The alternatives to engaging in the hard work required by this element of exegesis are too costly.

★ Chapter Summary

- The exegetical process includes the difficult but necessary task of discerning the historical, social, and cultural contexts of the text.

- Analyzing the literary context of a text means asking where the text is situated in its nearer as well as larger contexts.

- Considering the rhetorical context means asking why a text is where it is and what effect it has on readers/ hearers by virtue of its location.

- A text without a context is a pretext.

↖ Practical Hints

1. When considering the historical, social, and cultural contexts, which can encompass a vast quantity of information, always ask yourself, "Of everything I could learn and say about these contexts, what are the key facts and issues related to this passage that will affect my interpretation of it?" In writing a paper, eliminate, or at least greatly abridge, all other data.

2. When considering the literary and rhetorical contexts, again ask yourself, "What do I need to know and to say (in a paper) about the literary and rhetorical situation of the text that will affect my understanding of the text itself?"

👁 For Further Insight and Practice

1. Isaiah 9:1–7, which contains the words "For unto us a child is born," is celebrated in Handel's oratorio *Messiah* and is read especially during the Christmas season as a prophecy of the birth of Jesus. Skim the first nine chapters of Isaiah and/or consult a one-volume Bible commentary to find some information about the original historical context of this eighth-century B.C.E. text.

   (This assignment, by the way, raises the very significant question of how much the meaning of a biblical text is "tied" to, or dependent on, its original context.)

2. Read Mark 3:1–6, a story early in the narrative of Mark's Gospel that ends shockingly with the Pharisees plotting to kill Jesus. Then read carefully Mark 1–2 (and other parts of Mark, if time allows) and a Bible dictionary or encyclopedia article on the Pharisees. Based on your reading, explain in a few paragraphs the importance of the literary and social contexts for understanding the intense

conflict between the Pharisees and Jesus that is portrayed in this story.

3. Review chapter 11, section 4, pp. 166–70, "Resources for Contextual Analysis."

4. Read the sections on historical and literary contexts in the sample exegesis papers in the back of this book, Appendixes C and D.

CHAPTER FIVE

Formal Analysis

THE THIRD ELEMENT

The Form, Structure, and Movement of the Text

> Let chaos storm!
> Let cloud shapes swarm!
> I wait for form.
> —*Robert Frost*

> "It is impossible to play any game without
> a thorough knowledge of the laws that govern
> it, and you are at fault in making the attempt."
> —*Emily Post,* Etiquette, *chapter 31,*
> *"Games and Sports"*

What is the literary form of this text?

What is the literary genre of the document within which the text is situated?

How is the passage structured?

How does the text "move" from beginning to end?

Many people, especially when reading casually, simply "jump into" a text, whether it is a newspaper article, a book, a fund-raising appeal, or a love letter. If, however, a reader merely reads each of the words, sentences, or paragraphs individually, without paying attention to how the whole piece is put together, it is quite possible to "miss the forest for the trees." Moreover, as we know from daily experience, different kinds of reading material must be read with different principles of interpretation in mind, like the rules of a game.

In this chapter, we consider the form and shape of texts. We will look at how biblical texts are put together. This involves considering the type of writing that the text itself is as well as the type of writing within which it is found. It also involves studying the text's structure and its "movement" from start to finish. As one literary critic puts it, elements of design—structure, patterns, and so on—manifest both the artistic beauty of a text and its function or intended impact.[1] The general term we will use for the careful consideration of the literary form, structure, and movement of a text is *formal analysis*.

Form

Formal analysis begins with the question of the "form" of the passage. The terms *form, literary form,* and *genre* all refer to the *type* of literature that a particular text is. A literary form or genre is a set of texts with common, distinctive features. Most people prefer to use the term *genre* only for larger literary units and the term *form* or *literary form* for smaller units. In each case, however, the principle is the same: with respect to format, or formal features, much writing shares common traits with other pieces of writing. For our purposes, we must consider both the specific question of the form of the text being analyzed and the broader question of the literary genre of the writing in which the text appears.

From common experience, we realize that it is important to know the literary form or genre of a text because its form or genre affects the way we read and interpret the text. For instance, when we read a newspaper, we recognize (consciously or unconsciously) that the front-page news, the funnies, Ann Landers, the advertisements, and the editorials are different types of literature and must be interpreted as

---

[1] Ryken, *Words of Delight*, 91.

such. We understand, even if unconsciously, that each type of literature in a newspaper has its own characteristics as well as its own rules of interpretation. We expect an editorial to editorialize, and we look for it; we do not expect it, however, in a front-page news story. We allow for hyperbole in advertising; we do not tolerate it in the crime reports.

The Bible is not, from one perspective, truly a single book; it is a library. The books of the Bible exist in many different genres (for example, historical narratives; collections of hymns, proverbs, visions, and oracles; and letters[2]), and within the books there is also a wide variety of forms (for example, short stories, poems, parables, proverbs, sermons, laws). Responsible readers of the Bible must attempt to identify the literary form and genre of the texts they study and to understand the principles of interpretation that govern each type. To do anything less is to confuse the comics with the op-ed page.

Exegesis, because it focuses on a relatively short text, is more concerned about the form of that particular text than the genre of the document in which it is found. Nevertheless, the question of genre cannot be ignored. We need to ask:

- What kind of writing is this document?

- Are there general principles for the interpretation of this kind of writing that need to be employed?

For example, people wreak all kinds of havoc in the interpretation of the books of Daniel and Revelation when they do not realize that these are *apocalyptic* writings that freely use lavish symbolism and need to be read more like poetry than historical narrative.

Once you have determined the literary genre of the document—and some research may be needed to make the determination and consider how that affects interpretation—you are ready to look at the form of your specific

---

[2] There are even several types of letters and letter fragments in the Bible—letters of friendship, letters of recommendation, parenetic (advice) letters, and so on.

passage. The first question to ask about literary form is, Is the passage *prose* or *poetry?* If prose, is it a historical narrative? a symbolic narrative? a short story or tale? a parable? a miracle story? a speech? part of a letter?

If it is a speech or part of a letter, is the passage an argument? definition? explanation? moral instruction? apology (self-defense)?

If the text appears to be poetry (literature full of images and structured in segments called "verses" or "strophes"), does it just contain some rhythmic or poetic language, or is it actually a poem or hymn? (Note that biblical poetry is often called "thought rhyme," meaning poetry consisting of parallel phrases that are similar to or opposite of each other in meaning.) If it is a hymn or psalm, what kind of hymn is it (possibilities include praise, instruction, confession, and lament)?

Your answer to these questions will affect the way you read and interpret the text. Just as you do not read and interpret the various parts of a newspaper in the same way, you should not read a poem in the same way you read a prose historical narrative! Once you determine the literary type, you must approach the details of the text in an appropriate way, especially taking care, for instance, not to interpret symbolic language (for example, "the face of God" or "the lamb that was slain") literally.

Structure

After many years of reading and writing various kinds of literature (including student essays and research papers), I have become absolutely convinced that the key to good writing is organization, and the key to good reading is discovering that organization. On many occasions, after contemplating and applying the material in this chapter on form, structure, and movement, students have said: "It's all so clear now. The rest is easy. Once you see the structure, the movement, you understand the whole thing." This is often true. On the other hand, sometimes structure, like beauty, is in the eye of the beholder. The rest of this chapter should therefore be studied very carefully.

Some writing may appear to be done rather haphazardly, and sometimes that is in fact the case. Most writers, however, whether consciously or unconsciously, write with some kind of organizing principle or pattern that appears in their writing. The pattern or principle may be inherited from the writing conventions of the culture (as it often is), or it may be unique to the writer, or it may be (and very often is) a combination of tradition and creativity. Very few kinds of writing, and very few writers, are basically incoherent. There is meaning and purpose to a writer's activity and thus to the final product—the text itself. Discerning the structure that expresses this purposeful activity is, of course, challenging and—as one might expect—often more art than science.

Formal analysis includes consideration not only of the general form of a text but also its specific structure and movement. We are interested here, not in the structure of the biblical book as a whole (that has to do with context), but with the structure of the passage itself that is the focus of the exegesis. The *structure* of a passage refers to its parts, its main divisions and subdivisions, while the *movement* of a passage refers to the progression of the text, through those parts, from beginning to end. This section of your study is like a road map from AAA: the divisions of the text correspond to the main points of interest along your route, and the description of the text's movement corresponds to the routemaker's commentary on the scenery and road conditions between the points of interest.

The notion of a road map may sound a bit pedestrian (no pun intended!). A text, however, can be a beautiful thing, a work of art. To discern its structure is, in part, to pay attention to its literary beauty, to the aesthetics of the text. Discerning structure and movement is one function of rhetorical analysis or criticism, because rhetoric is sometimes defined as "literary artistry." A careful reader will be sensitive not only to the location of a text (context) but also to the formulation of the text itself (structure and movement). Both aspects of the text contribute to the meaning, beauty, and effectiveness of the text—that is, to its rhetorical power.

OUTLINES

Many students have found it very helpful to construct a phrase outline of a biblical text with one or two levels, so as to discern and express the text's structure and movement. Further subdivisions are not always necessary but can be helpful. The purpose of these phrase outlines is not merely to repeat the words of the text but to *summarize* their content and, if possible, their purpose or function in the passage. When constructing an outline, you should indicate which verses of the text correspond to each part of the outline.

The first part of an outline from a hypothetical text in one of the prophets might look like this:

    I. Condemnation of injustice (vv. 3–7)
      A. Hatred for the poor (vv. 3–4)
      B. Mistreatment of orphans and widows (vv. 5–6)
      C. Use of unfair scales (v. 7)
    II. Announcement of God's wrath (vv. 8–10)
    III. Plea for repentance (vv. 11–12)

An outline of the Disciples' (Lord's) Prayer from Matthew 6 might be done this way:

    I. Disciples' address to God as personal yet holy (v. 9)
      ("Our Father who art in heaven")
    II. Disciples' praise (v. 9) ("hallowed . . .")
    III. Disciples' prayer for the world (v. 10)
      ("Thy kingdom come, thy will be done on earth . . .")
    IV. Disciples' prayer for themselves (vv. 11–13)
      ("Give us this day . . . forgive us . . . lead us . . .")

COMMON STRUCTURAL PATTERNS

Discovering a structure or outline or organizational pattern in a text is, as noted above, something of an art. There is seldom only one "right answer," one correct way to outline a text; two people may discern two different, but equally legitimate, patterns in the text. It is helpful to know, however, that there are several common structural patterns that occur in many biblical texts; indeed, they occur in many texts outside the Bible, too.

Perhaps the most basic structural pattern of human communication is *repetition*. Repetition of a key word, phrase, or grammatical feature can be a clue not only to the structure of a text but also to the central concern of that text, as we will note again in chapter 7 on synthesis. The repetition of a previous element is sometimes an exact repetition and sometimes an allusion or briefer mention of some concept. We may refer to the fundamental pattern of repetition as AXAYAZ, in which X, Y, and Z are those sections not comprised of repeated material. If repetition occurs at structured intervals in a text, especially a longer text, it can be called a refrain (as in a poem or hymn).

Another simple but common structural pattern of expression is *contrast* or *antithesis*. The contrast may be between ideas, actions, characters, times (e.g., past and present), or other elements of human experience and expression. We may refer to this pattern as A [-A] for "A and the opposite of A." For example:

> So then, remember that *at one time* you Gentiles by birth . . . were *at that time* without Christ, being aliens from the commonwealth of Israel. . . . *But now* in Christ Jesus you who *once* were *far off* have been brought near by the blood of Christ. (Ephesians 2:11–13, NRSV)

A specialized form of both repetition and contrast that is very common in the Bible is *parallelism*—the expression of similar, related, or contrasting things set in parallel ways. As noted earlier, it is often said that biblical poetry is "thought rhyme," or parallelism. The Psalms, for instance, are often structured as a set of extended synonyms and/or antonyms, one line being followed by a restatement or development of it, or else the antithesis to it:

> Wash me thoroughly from my iniquity,
> And cleanse me from my sin. (Psalm 51:2, NRSV)

> [T]he LORD watches over the way of the righteous,
> but the way of the wicked will perish. (Psalm 1:6, NRSV)

It is not only a sentence or verse that may be structured in parallel (synonymous or antithetical) form but also an entire text or a segment of the text. We may refer to this as the A//A' pattern.

Another form of parallelism commonly marks the opening and closing of a text, thus indicating that what is in the middle is all interconnected. In many texts, either a word, phrase, image, or idea both introduces and concludes a paragraph or a stanza, a story or an argument. As noted in chapter 2, this phenomenon of beginning and ending on the same note is known as *inclusio* ("inclusion"). It can be illustrated by Psalm 8, which starts and finishes on the exact same note of praise: "O LORD, our Sovereign, how majestic is your name in all the earth" (vv. 1, 9, NRSV), or Romans 5:1–11, in which the inclusio is clear even though the words are not an exact repetition:

> Therefore, since we are *justified* by faith, we have peace with God *through our Lord Jesus Christ,* through whom we have obtained access to this grace in which we stand; and we *boast* in our hope of sharing the glory of God. . . . But more than that, we even *boast* in God *through our Lord Jesus Christ,* through whom we have now received *reconciliation.* (Romans 5:1–2, 11, NRSV)

We may refer to this as an ABA' pattern. The beginning and the ending elements function like bookends around the rest of the text.

Sometimes a text characterized by inclusio is further structured in parallel fashion from both ends, so that the second element of the text is somehow parallel to the next-to-last element. We may refer to this as an ABB'A' pattern. This structural pattern, also noted briefly in chapter 2, is known as *chiasmus,* from the Greek letter *chi,* which looks like an English *X.* Chiasmus in short texts looks like the following, whence the reference to the *X* or *chi* shape that can be drawn if the A elements are joined by a line and the B elements are similarly joined, as in Psalm 51:1 (NRSV):

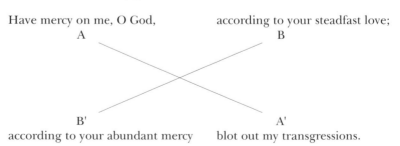

Have mercy on me, O God,   according to your steadfast love;
      A   B

      B'   A'
according to your abundant mercy   blot out my transgressions.

Also like an *X*, a longer text that is chiastically structured has two or more parallel elements at its "top" and "bottom." This pattern may continue, moving in (so to speak) from both ends, for the entirety of the text, so that the text appears to have a complex and complete parallel structure of, for example, ABCDEE'D'C'B'A'. Sometimes this is referred to as a *concentric* arrangement of the text or *ring composition*.

The chiastic or concentric pattern often has one solitary element of the text in the center, an element that has no parallel element; this pattern may be represented as ABCB'A', in which the C element in the chiastic ABCB'A' is the focal point, center of gravity, and fulcrum of the text as a whole. As in concentric patterns, it is possible for this structure to occur with many parallel elements hinging on one middle focal point. For example, the text from Romans 5 cited above may actually be structured chiastically:

A   Justification by faith, peace with God through Christ (vv. 1–2a)

B   Hope for glory (vv. 2b–5)

C   Christ's death as the manifestation of God's love (vv. 6–8)

B'   Certain hope of future salvation (vv. 9–10)

A'   Reconciliation with God through Christ (v. 11)

As we noted in chapter 2, some students of human language and thought believe that all human expression is naturally concentric or chiastic, having a beginning, a middle, and an end with several parallel elements on either side of the middle. In fact, some biblical commentaries propose that all the units of a biblical book, from the smallest to the largest—including the book itself—are structured chiastically.[3] The motto of other scholars is "a little bit of chiasmus goes a

---

[3] For example, Norman Gottwald outlines the entirety of Isaiah 56–66, or Third Isaiah, chiastically (*The Hebrew Bible: A Socio-literary Introduction* [Philadelphia: Fortress, 1985], 508). Peter F. Ellis does the same with the Gospel of John and all of its subparts (*The Genius of John: A Composition-Critical Commentary on the Fourth Gospel* [Collegeville, Minn.: Liturgical, 1984]).

long way." Sometimes two chiastic outlines of the same text, even a relatively small text, will indicate two very different center points and thus yield two very different readings of the text.

Many texts probably do possess a loose chiastic structure, being marked by inclusio and a clear center point, without having a one-for-one correspondence of all the elements on either side of the middle. The best guideline is probably to be alert to the likelihood of some kind of parallelism in every text and then to proceed carefully to look for signs of synonymous and antithetical parallelism, inclusio, and concentrism or chiasmus, but without forcing a text into following any of those patterns or into following them exactly and consistently.

There are of course other general ways that texts, whether ancient or modern, can be structured. For example, an introductory thought, image, or character can be developed or revealed in some systematic or unsystematic way. My own experience with texts suggests that careful study of most texts will reveal some structural pattern, even if the pattern is only that of a series of loosely related aspects of one central item.

PATTERNS COMMON TO CERTAIN LITERARY FORMS

In addition to generic structural patterns that may occur in any text, many literary genres follow somewhat regular patterns. Space permits only a few examples.

Exposition

Expository or argumentative writing, whether ancient or modern, usually sets out a thesis, for which support of various kinds is offered. The support may include arguments for the thesis itself as well as arguments against the opposite of the thesis (its antithesis).

As noted in the first chapter, rhetoric is the art of effective speaking and writing. Ancient rhetoric often followed a regular pattern:

- **introduction**—defining the speaker and topic *(exordium)*

- **narration** of relevant events *(narratio)*

- **thesis** or proposition *(propositio)*

- **arguments** for the thesis *(probatio)*

- **refutation** of counterarguments *(refutatio)*

- **recapitulation and appeal** *(peroratio)*

Within this standard pattern speakers or writers might insert other major elements (such as the *digressio,* or digression) and sprinkle various standard tools of the trade, such as appeals to reason *(logos),* emotion *(pathos),* tradition, authority (including sacred texts), and analogy. A text may be structured according to the formal rhetorical pattern as well as these various material elements.

Narrative

Although stories may convey a thesis or argument, that is not normally their primary intent, and they do not follow the structure of a piece of rhetoric. But stories, or narratives, do generally follow a predictable format: they always have a beginning, a middle, and an end. Within this basic structure they normally follow a pattern of "rising and falling action" that may be pictured as follows:

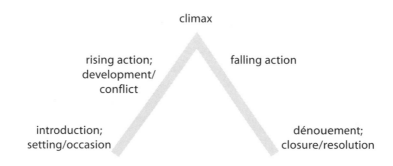

climax

rising action; development/ conflict

falling action

introduction; setting/occasion

dénouement; closure/resolution

An example of this sequence may be found in Mark 3:1–6
(NRSV):

> He looked around at them with
> anger; he was grieved at their hard-
> ness of heart and said to the man,
> "Stretch out your hand." He stretched
> it out, and his hand was restored.

They [the Pharisees] watched him to see
whether he would cure him on the sabbath, so that they might accuse him. And
he said to the man who had the withered
hand, "Come forward." Then he said to
them, "Is it lawful to do good or to do
harm on the sabbath, to save life or
to kill?" But they were silent.

The Pharisees went out . . .

Again he [Jesus] entered the
synagogue, and a man was there
who had a withered hand.

. . . and immediately conspired
with the Herodians against
him, how to destroy him.

Part of the brilliance of this story, of course, is that the ending does not fully resolve the conflict but invites the reader
to "stay tuned" for more. Thus this story is undoubtedly one
episode of rising action and conflict within a greater narrative in the Gospel of Mark as a whole, the climax of which
has not yet been reached.

Narratives are comprised of three basic kinds of text segments: narration of action, speech, and commentary. The
way these segments are arranged helps to define the structure of a narrative text.[4]

Specific kinds of narratives may display particular structures.
For instance, healing stories such as those recorded in the
gospels often follow this pattern: description of illness;
request for healing/expression of faith; narrative of healing;
reaction from person healed, crowd, and/or opponents.

---

[4] For typical story patterns, or archetypal plot motifs, see
Ryken, *Words of Delight*, 49.

A text being studied exegetically may encompass all or part of one of these patterns. For example, your text may be the *propositio* in a rhetorical piece of writing, or it may be the presentation of the conflict in a narrative. On the other hand, a text may tell a complete miracle story that simultaneously is both a full narrative, from introduction to dénouement, and a *narratio* within a larger rhetorical work. For emphasis, drama, or other effect, the writer may not only adopt a typical structural pattern but also adapt it. Furthermore, a text may follow both a structural pattern common to its literary form and one of the patterns of repetition, contrast, or parallelism discussed above.

Movement

The way a writer uses or alters the structural patterns is often very significant, and the resulting structure indicates also the *movement* of the text from beginning to end. There are, of course, many ways in which a passage can move from beginning to end. Some common general patterns and an example of each are:

- **description**—identification to details; Leviticus 25:1–7, the Sabbatical Year

- **exposition**—sequence of ideas or emotions; Isaiah 1:2–20, the divine lawsuit

- **repetition**—Deuteronomy 27:11–26, the Mosaic covenantal curses

- **logic**—if *or* since . . . then; Romans 6, the consequences of baptism

- **catalogue**—list; Galatians 5:19–23, works of the flesh and fruit of the Spirit

- **comparison/contrast**—Hebrews 9:1–14, the two sacrifices[5]

To discover the structure and movement of a text, it is especially helpful to look for key words that express the main

---

[5] Adapted from Ryken, *Words of Delight,* 209.

ideas and the relationships between the main ideas. For the main ideas, look principally at the main subjects and verbs; for relationships, look especially at words that indicate relationships between actions or ideas. These include such words as "next," "then," "while," "but," "therefore," "for," "because," "although," "in order that," and so on. (This process of looking at the relationships between parts of a text is described more fully in the next chapter on detailed analysis.) Look also for any evidence of repetition and/or contrast, or "theme and variation" or "point and counterpoint." As always, the discoveries made in looking at the details affect the understanding of the structure of the whole, and vice versa—such is the nature of exegesis as a hermeneutical circle.

In the typical healing story outlined above, the movement is from illness to faith to wholeness to, perhaps, praise by some and hatred by others. Other kinds of stories may also move from bad to good by the time of the dénouement (known in literature as "comedy"), like the story of Joseph or the narratives of Jesus' death and resurrection. Stories can also move from good to ill ("tragedy"), like the narratives of Adam and Eve, the fall of King Saul, and Jesus' suffering and death (apart from the resurrection).

Hymns (like the psalms) move from contemplation to praise or to complaint, from self-examination to confession, from fear to hope, and so on. Other texts may present a thesis, followed by pieces of evidence, culminating in a warning or instruction. Still others may present a command followed by a promise for those who obey, or describe a problem and offer a solution.

In an exegesis paper, it is helpful to writer and reader alike if the paper includes a brief phrase outline that indicates the basic content of each of the parts that a student discerns in the text.[6] (See the examples above of the fictional prophetic text and the Lord's Prayer.) The outline should be

---

[6] For more guidelines for writing a research exegesis paper, see Appendix B.

followed by a short statement of the movement of the text. This outline of the biblical passage becomes the outline for the detailed analysis of the text, which is the next part of the paper. Although consideration of form, structure, and movement takes much time in study and preparation, it should take up relatively little space in the paper. Otherwise (and this is a common problem) the paper becomes repetitious. However, if you have done a good job analyzing the structure and movement of the text, *your work is nearly half over*—in part because you have already been forced to begin the work of detailed analysis!

★ Chapter Summary

- The formal analysis of a text refers to the consideration of its literary form, its structure (divisions and subdivisions), and its movement from beginning to end.

- There are particular principles of interpretation appropriate to every literary form and genre.

- Common general structural patterns include repetition, contrast or antithesis, parallelism, inclusio, and chiasmus.

- Some literary forms and genres have common structural patterns specific to the genre, including such comprehensive genres as rhetorical speech and narrative, as well as specific forms such as miracle stories.

- Some general ways in which a text can move from beginning to end include description, exposition, repetition, logic, catalogue, and comparison/contrast.

↖ Practical Hints

1. Some basic literary genres, and the principles of interpretation that accompany them, are common from culture to culture, reflecting universal human ways of communication. Therefore, draw on your experience with literature and life generally as you read a text carefully with respect to its literary and rhetorical shape.

2. Become familiar with the basic literary forms in the Bible. Some suggested books on this topic are listed in chapter 11, section 5, pp. 170–72, "Resources for Formal Analysis."

3. The best way to discern the structure and movement of a text with any degree of precision is to "play with" the text on paper. This can be done by circling and underlining portions and marking connections you perceive, by re-writing the text phrase-by-phrase in outline form, or by creating some other kind of visual representation of the text as a whole.

👁 For Further Insight and Practice

1. Carefully read Psalm 19. What kind of literature is this? Compose a brief outline of the three or four major sections of the psalm, indicating their basic content. Describe in two or three sentences the movement of the psalm.

2. Read the brief but powerful narrative in Acts 9:1–9 about Saul, known later as Paul the apostle. (To understand the immediate context, skim Acts 6–7 and read carefully Acts 8:1–4.) What kind of literature is this? Describe the structure and movement of the story.

3. Compose an outline of the parts or "scenes" in the story of the golden calf in Exodus 32. Try to correlate the scenes you identify with the five stages of a typical narrative sequence described in this chapter. Describe the movement of the story and how this movement gives shape to the various characters in the story.

4. Describe the form, structure, and movement of Isaiah 1:21–31.

5. Review chapter 11, section 5, pp. 170–72, "Resources for Formal Analysis."

6. Carefully read the sections on form, structure, and movement in the sample exegesis papers, Appendixes C and D.

CHAPTER SIX

Detailed Analysis of the Text

The Fourth Element

"It is not in the interest of extravagant ambition
that we trouble ourselves with this detailed exposition, but we hope through such painstaking interpretation to train you in the importance of not
passing over even one slight word or syllable in
the Sacred Scriptures. For they are not ordinary
utterances, but the very expression of the Holy
Spirit, and for this reason it is possible to find
great treasure even in a single syllable."
—*John Chrysostom*

***What are the main points of each of the
parts of the text, and how does the text/
the writer make these points?***

***What do the details mean in the big picture,
and how does the big picture affect the
meaning of the details?***

In some respects, detailed analysis is the very heart of exegesis. It is what an exegete is all about: careful scrutiny
of every word, phrase, allusion, grammar point, and syntactical feature in the text. Opening randomly to the
middle of almost any biblical commentary, you will likely
discover discussion of details. In this chapter we will
explore various aspects of performing an in-depth analysis of the text.

The Pieces of a Puzzle

Attention to detail is indeed the stuff of commentaries and the heart of exegesis. Nevertheless, a shift in commentary writing, and in scholarly understanding of exegesis, occurred in the last twenty-five years or so of the twentieth century. Many earlier commentaries took a very narrow, word-by-word, phrase-by-phrase approach that did not give much attention to the larger units of thought or the contexts in which the words and phrases appear. The danger of these commentaries was missing the big picture. Most recent commentaries place a great deal of emphasis on the form, structure, and context of texts as a way of interpreting the meaning of the details.

The beginning exegete may face the same temptation to which older commentaries succumbed. Overwhelmed by the quantity of words in the text, the numbers of questions these words raise, and (eventually) the extraordinary amount of scholarly ink spilled over every jot and tittle of the text, you can easily get so bogged down in the details that you miss the big picture. This is not to say that the details can be dealt with casually or ignored—quite the opposite! But the careful interpreter is always asking the question, "What do these details mean in the big picture, and how does the big picture affect the meaning of the details?" This is the hermeneutical circle at work.

In some ways, exegesis is like doing a puzzle. To put together a puzzle, you must find and arrange the small pieces (details) in order to create a picture (the whole). The process involves identifying the parts and discovering how they fit together. Without the little pieces, there would be no puzzle picture. But the little pieces alone are only a very small part of the picture; their ultimate value lies in their contribution to the larger picture.

THE ART OF SELECTIVITY

As mentioned in the last chapter, the detailed explanation of the content of a passage follows the outline of the text devised for the previous step, the formal analysis (form, structure, and movement). The detailed analysis is therefore logically divided into two or more (usually three to five) sections corresponding to the major parts of the outline. In these sections, you carefully examine (and discuss, if you are writing a paper), the key ideas of each segment of the text.

This section of a written exegesis can become very long if every phrase of the text is analyzed. That is precisely what you will find in scholarly commentaries, some of which contain a thousand pages or more on one biblical book. In your investigation of the text, first on your own and then in researching the work of others, you must observe and analyze as much as you possibly can. Like a detective, attempt to leave no stone unturned, no question unexplored.

In writing an exegesis paper, however, you must be *selective*, commenting in detail only on the most significant features of each verse in the passage, making more concise observations about other features, and ignoring still others. Deciding what is and is not important is partly a matter of intuition, partly a matter of overall careful study of the text and its contexts, and partly a matter of experience. Once again, the hermeneutical circle will be at work. As you carefully engage the details of a text, an understanding of the whole passage will begin to emerge. As it does, you will begin to have a feel for what elements of the text deserve the most attention and emphasis in an exegesis paper (or, for that matter, in a homily or sermon). Exegesis of a text, even when using appropriate historical and literary methods, is more like an art than a science.

Some Basic Questions

Every genre, indeed every passage, of the Bible is unique. Still, there are some basic questions about every passage that you need to ask yourself. Examples of these fundamental questions are:

- What does the text communicate, and how?

- What are the key terms and images? What do they mean?

- Are there any key terms or ideas whose meaning may be explained by looking elsewhere in the book?

- Are there any literary or rhetorical devices (simile, metaphor, hyperbole, personification, repetition, irony, etc.), and if so, what is their effect?

- What kinds of sentences are used? What are the major components of each sentence? What verbal actions or states appear in these sentences, and what subjects are associated with them?

- Does the text include appeals to tradition or Scripture, such as stories, beliefs, laws, and well-known historical figures? If so, how do these appeals function?

- Does the text appear to use any other earlier sources, whether written or oral? If so, how are the sources used?

- If the text is a narrative, what elements of setting, plot (conflict, suspense, resolution), and character development does each part of the text, and the text as a whole, convey?

- Which elements of the text work, individually or together, to instruct, delight, or move the reader?

- What is the tone, or mood, of the passage, and what elements convey that tone?

- How do the various parts of the passage reflect and/or address the situation of the readers?

- How does each part of the passage relate to the other parts?

- How does each part contribute to the whole?

- How does my emerging understanding of the whole affect the meaning of the parts?

This is a broad range of questions, and more could be added to the list. Some of these questions are directed primarily at each part (word, sentence, etc.) of the entire text. Others are directed at the text as a whole. Readers who ask and answer these kinds of questions will have much to say about a text.

These questions may, in fact, be sufficient for this element of the exegetical process. The rest of the chapter, however, provides more detailed guidance on the task of detailed analysis. Specifically, we will look at what the various parts of a text are and at how the parts relate to one another. Then we will consider some important aspects of the text as a whole, especially in light of the sources it may contain and/or use.

The Whole and the Parts

A text obviously exists as a whole, as a "relatively self-contained unit of meaning," but it also consists of numerous parts. The units of meaning that an exegete will normally analyze, from the smallest to the largest, are the following:

- **words**—lexical items

- **sentence segments**—phrases

- **sentences**—or utterances

- **text segments**—paragraphs, stanzas, and smaller clusters of sentences

- **the text itself**—as a whole

What these various units of meaning have in common, apart from words, is that each has a sort of completeness: each is a unit of meaning with a beginning and end. They differ with respect to size and degree of completeness and thus with respect to the kind and quantity of meaning they convey. Students of language generally view the sentence, or utterance, as the basic unit of meaningful, complete communication, what we sometimes refer to as a "complete thought." Sentences usually consist of phrases, which are made up of words. Sentences work together, so to speak, to form larger segments of a text, and the segments combine to form the text (sometimes called the "discourse") itself.

The process of exegesis works, as we have seen, as a hermeneutical circle, a back-and-forth movement between one dimension of the text and another—in this case, between the whole and the parts. One can begin the process of detailed analysis in several ways—with key words or phrases, for instance, or with sentences. Eventually, every part of the text needs to be examined. In the presentation of one's exegesis in a paper, however, the procedure is normally to work systematically segment by segment, within each segment to work sentence by sentence (which often means verse by verse), within each sentence to examine each phrase, and within each phrase to analyze each key word.

Since many people are fascinated with the smallest unit of meaning in the Bible, the word, we will begin our discussion of the parts with it. The amount of detailed analysis of a text and its words will be dependent upon the length of the paper.

Key Words and Images

One of my best teachers of exegetical method used to urge us to treat every key word or image (word-picture) in the text like an unknown variable—the x or y—of an algebra equation. For example, in examining the following verse we should clearly treat the italicized words, and perhaps others, as such unknown variables:

> And the *Word* became *flesh* and *lived* among us, and we have seen his *glory*, the glory as of a *father*'s *only son*, full of *grace* and *truth*. (John 1:14, NRSV)

The suggestion to treat key words as unknown variables is good advice, but some caution is needed in analyzing these words as "lexical items" or "dictionary entries." What scholars sometimes call "lexical analysis" and others "word studies" is an area of exegesis full of potential land mines. The following discussion suggests why this is true and how to avoid the dangers of "word studies."

MEANING IN CONTEXT

Many people assume that words are the most important conveyors of meaning. Both modern linguistics and ordinary experience, however, teach us that meaning is context-dependent. The exclamation "Oh, my God!" has one meaning in the context of praying and quite another in the context of admiring someone's new car. Popularly, people recognize that a word's denotation ("literal" meaning) and its connotation (implied or suggested meaning) can differ, and that a word can mean different things to different people and in different social locations or contexts.

Linguists suggest that although a word, or lexical item, may have some core features, it has a spectrum of possible meanings, called its semantic range. The meaning or function of the item depends on a variety of factors, but especially on the various contexts in which it occurs. These contexts include especially the speaker's or writer's social location, his or her personal word bank and style (i.e., what does this person normally mean when using this term?), and the literary and rhetorical setting in which the term appears. What is the speaker or writer trying to accomplish, and how does this term serve those purposes? A word has a range of "dictionary" or commonly recognized meanings (lexical senses), only one of which is its meaning *in context* (contextual sense). Furthermore, if a person or group uses a word for particular purposes and invests its own meaning into the word, it may take on a new and peculiar sense for that person or group (specialized sense).[1]

For example, the lexical sense of the word *fellowship* may be "association of people with common interests" or "specialized academic appointment with stipend." Its contextual sense in the sentence "The church is a fellowship" is clearly the former, not the latter. However, the general dictionary sense is further refined in its religious context and may, in some churches, take on a peculiar, specialized sense, as in "a time of fellowship after church." Here the specialized sense is "informal conversation with light refreshments"—and the conversation may not even be of a religious nature. Other churches would not use, or perhaps even understand, the term in that way.

---

[1] This is sometimes called a "technical term."

A "biblical" word, therefore, should not be treated as an unchanging, homogeneous unit of meaning. For example, the word *salvation* has different meanings among the various biblical writers. In the first instance, it probably does not mean exactly the same thing for Isaiah as it does for Matthew, even when Matthew is quoting Isaiah. And *salvation* may not mean the same thing for Matthew as it does for another New Testament writer such as Luke or Paul. It is even possible—and here is why context is so important—that one writer can use the same word differently in different contexts.

FURTHER PRINCIPLES FOR THE ANALYSIS OF WORDS

A biblical word, then, does not mean the same thing every place it occurs. Neither does a word ever mean everything it could possibly mean at one time. The erroneous notion that a word in a particular context means the sum total of all (or even some) of its possible meanings is called *illegitimate totality transfer,* a term coined by the British biblical scholar James Barr.[2] Illegitimate totality transfer occurs when, for example, a significant biblical term like *faith* or *salvation* is interpreted in a specific passage as the conglomeration of all meanings of the word in the Bible, not according to the usage of the author or according to the context. That kind of universal synthesis is bad exegesis.[3]

Nor, finally, does a word mean what its origin and history (etymology), or its component parts, might suggest. Words take on a life of their own (like texts!) and naturally break away from their roots. For example, the contemporary meaning of the word *enthusiasm* has nothing to do with "being in God," despite its roots in the Greek words for "in" *(en)* and "God" *(theos).* This common misinterpretation of words is called the *etymological fallacy.*

---

[2] James Barr, *The Semantics of Biblical Language* (Oxford: Oxford University Press, 1961), 218.

[3] One "translation" of the Bible, The Amplified Bible, is based on this thoroughly flawed understanding of language.

The meaning of a word, then, is dependent upon a combination of the dictionary meaning and the context. The importance of these various contextual principles may be illustrated by consideration of the word(s) *green + house*. Let us imagine for a moment that English, like ancient Greek, were written without breaks between the words, such that the two words *green house* and the single word *greenhouse* would both be written as *greenhouse*. If we came upon the word while reading a newspaper column about trends in exterior home decoration, we could probably assume that *green house* (two words) is meant. However, if we saw the word while reading a column about trends in plant care, we could probably assume that *greenhouse* (one word) is intended. In neither case, however, would we be correct to transfer the meaning from one context to the other (i.e, there is no new trend to grow plants in houses with green exteriors) or to add up the two meanings and conclude, for example, that people are starting to live in hothouses painted green. To draw either conclusion would be to engage in illegitimate totality transfer.

Similarly, it would be erroneous to suggest that the words *green house*, or even *greenhouse*, must have something to do with growth simply because the word *green* is related to the Old English verb "to grow." This error is an example of an etymological fallacy. If a green house or a greenhouse has anything to do with growth, it is due to factors other than the history of the word *green*.

When analyzing the key variables in the equation—the words—it is important to gather as much basic information about these main words as possible in order then to determine their meaning in context. This information would include the normal semantic range (possible meanings) of the word, as well as the usage of the word elsewhere in the particular book or writer. There are three main types of tools to assist in the interpretation of words: dictionaries, or lexicons; wordbooks that contain essays on important biblical words; and concordances, or alphabetically arranged indexes of biblical words. Of particular importance is the concordance, which can identify all the places where a word and its linguistic relatives ("cognates") occurs. Concordances and other lexical tools are discussed in section 6 of chapter 11.

CONNOTATION AND FIGURATIVE LANGUAGE

Two additional aspects of word usage that are important for exegesis may also be mentioned briefly here: connotation and figurative language, or imagery.

We all know that sometimes a word functions outside its normal semantic range. A word's "connotation," or what it suggests in a general cultural context or a particular rhetorical situation, is particularly difficult to grasp. Knowledge of the historical and social setting of a text is the only thing that can help. For example, many Americans think that they may summon a French waiter by calling "Garçon," but in contemporary France that term connotes disrespect for the server (even though a French-English dictionary might include "waiter" as one translation of "garçon"). The appropriate address nowadays is "Monsieur," even though most French-English dictionaries do not provide "waiter" as a translation of "Monsieur."

Figurative language is also a universal phenomenon. Sometimes images are very culturally conditioned, while others are more universal because they are based on universal human experiences (such as light and darkness). The Bible is full of evocative images. These words (and even phrases, sentences, and longer units) must be interpreted by means of a disciplined imagination in light of the context in which they appear. Readers should be particularly attentive to the presence and function of metaphors (e.g., "God is a rock") and similes (e.g., "God is like a rock") in the text. It is not unusual to find that the key term in a text is in figurative language. This is sometimes referred to as the *governing image* or the *ruling metaphor.* For example, the first half of Psalm 23 is governed by the image of the Lord as "my shepherd."

The Arrangement of Words into Larger Units (Phrases, Sentences, and Text Segments)

Words do not normally stand alone; they are arranged into larger groupings, which we may call phrases or sentence segments. The arrangement of words into phrases and of phrases into sentences is referred to as syntax. As noted above, the primary linguistic unit for expressing meaning is not the word or even the phrase but the sentence. Sentences, in turn, are arranged into larger units of thought and expression that can be called text segments, which may be as few as two sentences and as many as a dozen. Such larger text segments are called paragraphs (prose) or stanzas (poetry). Exegesis requires careful analysis of all of these units.

Phrases are ordered combinations of words that follow patterns of usage within themselves and in relationship to one another (rules of grammar and syntax). It is of course impossible to grasp all the nuances of Greek or Hebrew grammar and syntax in translation, so precise exegesis depends on in-depth knowledge of the original languages. Nevertheless, exegetes who do not read the original languages can still pay close attention to questions of syntax and sentence structure. The analysis of each verse or sentence can be begun by dividing it into its several segments: the noun phrase, the verb phrase, and any qualifying or expanding phrases such as prepositional or adverbial phrases, which perform a kind of "fine tuning" on the language of the text and are often crucial to the meaning and function of the text.

As you begin to think systematically about the several verses of your passage, you will start asking yourself such questions as:

- What are the main phrases in this text?

- How are these phrases related to one another?

- Is their order significant?

Once the phrases that contain the subject(s) and verb(s) are identified, it is also important to determine the type of verb(s) (action or state of being), as well as the tense (time), and mood (e.g., indicative [declarative] or imperative) of each. What is the significance of these aspects of the verbs? Are the verb tenses all the same, or are past, present, and future tenses mixed? If they are mixed, why?

Are there verb phrases that relate closely to each other? Are they coordinate phrases (equal partners), or is one subordinate to another? What word or other device indicates this relationship? How is the coordination or subordination important to the meaning of the text?

As for the sentences themselves, what kind are they? Each sentence will be either a declaration, an imperative (either command or counsel), a question, or an exclamation.[4] What is the type of each sentence, and what is the meaning of that sentence as a unit?

As these questions are addressed to the text, and tentative answers come to mind, it is helpful to create a two-column phrase chart. In such a chart, you write, or print out, the text phrase by phrase to the left side of the paper, skipping several lines between phrases. On the right side of the paper, opposite each phrase, you note your perception of the meaning and function of each phrase in the text. The following is an example, for just one verse:

Text phrase	Meaning and function
In the beginning	—adverbial phrase indicating time of action and (perhaps) the action to follow as the beginning of time
God created	—identifies subject and verb; limits creation to God alone; narrates character of God (creative)
the heavens and the earth	—two objects/products of creation; encompasses all of known reality

---

[4] Declarations, questions, and exclamations generally use verbs in the indicative mood, whereas imperatives generally employ verbs in the imperative mood (e.g., "He goes," "Does he go?" and "He is going!" versus "Go").

The sizes of the columns and rows can be adjusted as you add notes and expand and refine your own exegetical work. Creating this chart on a computer simplifies this modification process as you continue to think more systematically about the relationships that exist among the various parts. If you would like to do "sentence diagramming," you may wish to try it on part or all of the passage.[5]

The Interrelationships among the Parts

We have already considered the fact that exegesis is a "circular" endeavor, a process of moving back and forth between the parts and the whole (a "hermeneutical circle"). To understand a text, one must not only consider the meaning of each of the parts, but also of the parts to one another:

- What are the explicit and implicit relationships of the key words to one another? the phrases in each sentence?

- How do the sentences relate to one another?

- How do the sentences work together to become a larger unit of meaning? Are there any contradictions or discrepancies among the sentences?

Indeed, we must stress not only that meaning is dependent on context but also that meaning is dependent on *relationships*. Words, phrases, sentences, and so on do not have meaning in isolation but in relationship and in context. Some of these relationships are largely explicit, while others are largely implicit in nature.

EXPLICIT RELATIONSHIPS

There are several kinds of typical interrelationships that are largely explicit to look for among the various segments of a

---

[5] Some exegetical handbooks stress sentence diagramming, while others criticize it as a linguistically flawed approach to sentence analysis. My view is that it can be helpful but that a phrase chart like the one illustrated in the text is more accessible to most students and can serve equally well, if not better.

text. These relationships may exist, for instance, among the phrases of a sentence or among the sentences within a larger segment.

One obvious set of interrelationships sometimes indicated by phrases is the one that exists among the subjects, verbs, and other "participants" in the action of a sentence. For example, in the opening sentence of the Bible quoted above, one segment indicates the actor ("God"), another the action ("created"), and another the resulting product of the action ("the heavens and the earth"). (These interrelationships are sometimes indicated in biblical languages by grammatical forms, though the translation of those forms often requires phrases in English.)

In addition to these interrelationships, there are also, as noted above, phrases and sentences that expand or qualify other phrases or sentences. These segments of the text identify, define, describe, or limit other segments. In the example above, "In the beginning" qualifies the action with respect to time.

We may also distinguish between *chronological,* or *narrative,* relationships, on the one hand, and *logical* relationships on the other. The relationships are sometimes—though not always—indicated by verbal markers, including such narrative markers as "before, "while," and "after," and such logical markers as "because," "so that," "therefore," and "by" or "through." Chronological or narrative relationships among parts, and some of the markers,[6] include:

- **simultaneous action**—"while," "when"

- **prior action**—"before"

- **subsequent action**—"then," "next," "after this," "when"

- **reaction**—"then"

- **consequential action**—"therefore"

---

[6]The markers noted are English words. Obviously, the markers will be different words, or sometimes grammatical forms, in the original languages.

- **location of action/setting**—e.g., "on Zion"

- **time of action**—e.g., "on the third day"

Logical relationships among parts, and some common markers, include the following:

- **condition**—"if"

- **reason**—"because"

- **purpose**—"so that," "in order to"

- **result or consequence**—"therefore," "so that," "then"

- **means or instrumentality**—"by," "through"

- **concession**—"though," "although"

There are also some relationships that can be either chronological or narrative in character. These include comparison (similarity) and contrast (difference). It should also be noted that certain texts, such as the poetry of the psalms and certain of Paul's arguments, have both a logical and a narrative character to them.

IMPLICIT RELATIONSHIPS

Not all relationships among the parts of a text are explicit. For example, the reasons for a character's action or a writer's exhortation may not be stated. Careful analysis may be able to discern important connections that are not explicitly made in the text; in a paper, the existence of such connections must not only be asserted but also demonstrated.

According to some theories of language, relationships exist in every text between that which is said and the opposite of that which is said. Every assertion, in other words, implies the negation of something else. The Pauline acclamation "Jesus is Lord," for example, means that Paul is not Lord, Caesar is not Lord, and so on.

One form of the method known as "structural exegesis" assumes that every text contains an inherent pattern, or structure, of opposing convictions. Daniel Patte, the foremost practitioner of this method, seeks to identify both the various interrelated beliefs, or "faith convictions," expressed in a text and the explicit or implicit "oppositions" to those convictions. Patte and others look not only for what the author says but also for what the author means *not* to say. Thus these exegetes find contrasting subjects, actions, locations, and so on in every text, all related to a text's faith convictions and oppositions.

Looking for implicit contrasting relationships in a text can generate very significant insights. Exegetes must be careful, however, in drawing inferences about opposites, because sometimes two apparently opposite affirmations can both be true. The Pauline acclamation cited above, for instance, does *not* mean for Paul that "YHWH is not Lord"; in fact, quite the opposite is true. With this caution in mind, however, a good reader will always look for implicit relationships in a text, whether relationships of contrast or the kinds of chronological or logical relationships discussed above.

SUMMARY

The astute exegete will look carefully at the text to discern and describe its many interrelationships. Recording observations and questions allows the kind of "playing with the text" or "thinking on paper" that is necessary for careful close reading of the text.

Dimensions of the Text as a Whole

It is unlikely that most of the books of the Bible were written by one person at one sitting, or even over the course of time, without the use of prior sources, whether oral, written, or both. Quotations, allusions, and evidence of reliance on other materials abound in the Bible. The question for exegesis is, What do we do with these phenomena?

SOURCES AND REDACTION

The historical-critical method developed and flourished in large measure because scholars recognized discrepancies and disjunctures within texts. This led them to conclude that most biblical texts were like an onion, with many layers of literary and preliterary material buried within them, or like puzzles with various pieces fitted together, sometimes well and sometimes not so well. The purpose of the historical-critical method was and is, in large measure, to determine the origin, development, compilation, and editing of these various sources.

As noted in the first chapter, the tasks of the historical-critical method have specific names attached to them. *Source criticism* is the task of uncovering the various sources, especially written sources, that have been used within a text. *Form criticism* is the task of identifying small units within a text and classifying them with respect to type, or form (such as hymns, laments, etc.), that existed in either written or especially oral form before the text itself. Form critics also attempt to identify the kind of situation within Israel or early Christianity in which such a form would originate and prove useful. *Tradition criticism* is the discipline that seeks to identify the ways in which specific forms or oral traditions may have evolved as they were passed on from place to place and time to time. Though all of these criticisms focus on the preliterary and/or prefinal form of the text, *redaction criticism* is the discipline devoted to how the final "redactors," or editors of the Bible, adopted and adapted the various sources they had at their disposal for their own purposes. Redaction criticism also traces the writer's interests throughout the biblical book, as evidenced by trends and themes in the use of the sources. Some specific examples of the kind of questions these various criticisms address are listed in Appendix A.

Reactions to the historical-critical method, as defined by these criticisms, range from staunch defenders and practitioners, to uncompromising critics who assault its methodological presuppositions and/or theological value, to those who see its value but also its limitations and problems. This volume takes the last of these three positions.

No matter how one feels about the methods in principle, in practice they are difficult to execute. Without detailed knowledge of the original languages, not to mention ancient cultures and patterns of communication or early Israelite and Christian history, many of these criticisms simply cannot be carried out responsibly.

The one possible exception to this problem may be redaction criticism. If an exegete has good reason to suspect that a writer has used a source,[7] and the source can be identified, then by using the original languages, or even using a good translation, the average exegete can engage in redaction criticism with some degree of success. For instance, if the majority of scholars is correct and Matthew used both Mark and some other written source, called "Q," then we may be able to study how Matthew uses Mark to learn in part what Matthew wishes to highlight or play down in his Gospel.

Redaction criticism asks the following kinds of questions of a text:

- What evidence of sources is there in this text? Are there differences in vocabulary, style, and/or literary form? Are there "seams" or other problematic points in the flow of the narrative or logic? Is there an introductory formula indicating a quotation (e.g., "Moses says ...")?

- For what purpose has the writer used the source?

- How has the source been altered? Has it been abbreviated or expanded? Has it been rearranged? Have words or phrases been replaced by other words or phrases?

- Do these alterations seem to have an intended effect? Are they unusual for the writer or document, or are they consistent with other aspects of the writing in question?

The problems, of course, with redaction criticism are that (1) we cannot always know for sure that there was a source, (2) we can seldom know for sure why the source was used and changed, and (3) we cannot assume, if a writer uses a source, that any differences from the source are either intentional or significant. Moreover, even if the differences are deemed significant, we cannot conclude that the differ-

---

[7] For example, if it is the scholarly consensus or if the biblical writer quotes a known document.

ences represent the most important dimensions of the writer's literary or theological perspective. Furthermore, sometimes what redaction critics identify as seams or other evidence of sources and redaction, literary critics identify as literary or rhetorical devices.

Critics of redaction criticism stress the gravity of these problems and advocate exegesis of the final form of the text alone, as a literary whole. While exegesis of the final form of the text is the general approach taken in this book, it is important to acknowledge both that there are recognizable sources in the biblical writings and that, with care, the identification of these sources and the analysis of their use contribute to the exegesis of a text. In other words, proceed with caution! It would be a mistake to build a complete exegetical house of cards on a source theory, but it would be equally grievous to ignore quotations of and allusions to various sources in the Bible.

INTERTEXTUALITY

Recent study of the Bible and other literature has emphasized the reality that much of what people write is always a kind of weaving together of the new and the old. Human literary creativity almost always includes quotations and allusions to texts, ideas, and images from the culture in which it is nurtured. That is, texts contain echoes of other texts, as well as reverberations of additional linguistic items from the environment. This phenomenon is called *intertextuality,* and it permeates the Bible. As one scholar says, "the Bible itself is an intertextual fabric within which later texts elaborate on earlier texts."[8] For example, Isaiah 61 ("The spirit of the Lord GOD is upon me . . . he has sent me to bring good news to the oppressed"), probably written after the Babylonian exile, appears to echo Isaiah 42, probably written during the exile, and is clearly echoed by Luke

---

[8]Wim Weren, *Windows on Jesus: Methods in Gospel Exegesis* (trans. John Bowden; Harrisburg, Pa.: Trinity, 1999), 200.

in his account of Jesus' "inaugural sermon" at Nazareth (Luke 4:16–21).

If we limit the term intertextuality, as some scholars do, to mean the use of known written texts, then clearly the most important dimension of intertextuality for the New Testament is its hundreds of quotations of and allusions to the Scriptures (or Old Testament). Fortunately, many editions of the Bible indicate these in cross-references and notes. Even the books of the Old Testament, or Hebrew Bible, however, seem constantly to take up and refer to earlier texts or traditions (such as the exodus) that now are part of the Bible. While this may not always be intertextuality in the narrow sense of the word, the final product is clearly a woven fabric.

Thus, to ignore the Bible's quotations of and allusions to such texts, ideas, and images is to neglect one of the most significant aspects of almost any particular text. The meaning of many texts depends in part—and sometimes in large measure—on their "interaction" with other texts. For this reason, it is not merely the historical critic but also the literary critic and the average reader or exegete who must attend to the "sources"—defined in the broadest sense possible—that are woven into biblical texts.

One problem to avoid, however, is the error of what the Jewish biblical scholar Samuel Sandmel termed "parallelomania": the excessive hunt for parallels as sources for, or as points of contrast to, the biblical text.[9] Although there may be many allusions to or apparent quotations from other sources, this happens in part because a text, idea, or image is "in the air," part of the cultural pool of presuppositions. The wise exegete does not fall into the trap of thinking that similarity means either interdependence or deliberate citation. On the other hand, a direct scriptural quote by a New Testament writer should be understood for what it is and analyzed for how it has been used by the writer.

---

[9] Samuel Sandmel, "Parallelomania," *Journal of Biblical Literature* 81 (1962): 1–13.

Excursus: Narrative Detail

Since so much of the Bible is narrative literature, it requires some special attention. In some older discussions of exegesis, the term "literary criticism" meant the analysis of (literary) sources in a text—picking it apart, so to speak. Today literary criticism can mean many things (from the general study of the literary aspects of a text to the use of specialized literary theories), but it does not mean looking for the (earlier) components of a text. Rather, current interest is in the final form of a narrative text. The best term for this kind of analysis is *narrative criticism*. Narrative criticism is not interested in the original forms embedded in the text, its stages of development, or the purely editorial work of the supposed redactor. It is not inherently interested (though neither is it necessarily disinterested) in the actual community that produced the text. Narrative analysis deals with the story as story and with the author/narrator and reader/hearer that the text implies—which may not be synonymous with the actual writer and audience. (These are often referred to as the "implied author" and the "implied reader.") It deals with the final form of the text.

As noted in the chapter on form, structure, and movement, narrative literature follows a pattern of (1) introduction (setting, occasion), (2) rising action (development, conflict), (3) climax, (4) falling action, and (5) resolution (dénouement, closure). Together this sequence of elements forms the narrative's plot. The detailed analysis of a narrative text includes careful attention to which of these elements are present in the text (it may be some or all). It must also include consideration of other narrative elements of the text, such as character development. Who are the characters? How are they developed (through description? their actions?) What are their roles in the story—are they a protagonist (leading character), or an antagonist, or do they play a supporting role? Attention to invisible characters and forces (such as supernatural powers, including God) is crucial in the exegesis of many biblical narratives.

Astute exegetes will do everything in their power to enter the "narrative world" of the story. In light of the context of the narrative within the biblical book as a whole, try to imagine the setting, the characters, the interrelationships among the characters (including conflict), the mood and emotions that the story contains. How does the story begin? What is the climactic moment of the story? How does it end?

After doing this imaginative work, you will be better prepared to engage the story more critically and creatively. What aspects of setting are presented in the story and why? What elements of the story explicitly or implicitly depict characters and their interrelationships? What words, phrases, and sentences convey the mood of the story and its central motif or apparent purpose? How do the characters and actions within this narrative relate to other parts of the larger narrative of which this story or section is a part?

These and similar questions are the questions most of us learned to ask of literature in school. Some of us have not always been encouraged to ask them of biblical texts, but they can, indeed must, be asked. Two final points must be made, however. First, doing narrative criticism and intertextual analysis or even redaction criticism are not mutually incompatible. One may inquire both about how a text adopts and adapts other sources *and* how the text works together as a whole unit and as part of a larger literary entity. Second, doing narrative analysis of a text need not be restricted to texts that are obviously stories. Many texts that are poetic or expository in form contain a story within or behind them, complete with characters, conflict, and resolution. Other texts allude to stories or contain parts of large, master narratives, such as the story of God's salvation through the exodus or the cross and resurrection.

In some important sense, as many recent students of the Bible have suggested, much of the Bible is narrative literature, and the Bible as a whole tells a set of interrelated stories. The careful exegete will always be attentive to the elements of narrative in every biblical text, as well as the larger narratives to which the biblical texts persistently refer.

Conclusion

The quantity and character of questions to be considered and addressed in doing the detailed analysis of a text can be overwhelming. One should not, however, give up. For one thing, like doing anything else, exegesis requires practice. As the French say to convey the idea that "practice makes perfect," "C'est en forgeant que l'on devient forgeron": "It is by smithing that one becomes a blacksmith." Or, "It is only by doing exegesis that one becomes an exegete."

For another, the more you look, the more you will see. The story is told of a fifth-grade science teacher who once had her class stare at a frog in an aquarium. The students were supposed to record everything they observed. When they all thought they were done, she made them keep staring and recording. When she told them to put their pencils down, they all replied, "But we're not done."

★ Chapter Summary

- Exegesis involves balancing attention to the big picture and to the details.

- It is important to select carefully which details to analyze.

- There are some basic questions of detail to ask of every text concerning key words, images, literary devices, sentence components, appeals to tradition, sources, narrative and rhetorical elements, tone and mood, and the relation of the parts to the whole.

- The exegetical process is a hermeneutical circle, moving back and forth from the parts to the whole.

- Key words and images in a text are like unknown variables in an equation; their meaning is dependent on context and relationship to other elements.

- Careful analysis of the phrases in a text, and the function of each phrase, is an essential part of the exegetical process.

- The parts of the text have both explicit and implicit relationships to one another.

- Exegesis includes the attempt to identify any sources used by the text and *how* they are used.

- Exegesis must also address intertextuality, or the phenomenon of texts echoing other texts.

- Detailed analysis of narrative texts includes attention to plot, character development, and the "narrative world" of the text.

↖ Practical Hints

1. Recording observations and questions allows the kind of "playing with the text" or "thinking on paper" that is

necessary to careful close reading of the text. A two-column phrase chart, with the phrases of the text on the left and space for your observations on the right, may be especially helpful.

2. Constantly ask yourself, "What do these details mean in the big picture, and how does the big picture affect the meaning of the details?"

👁 For Further Insight and Practice

1. For an idea of the kinds of things you might want to discuss in an exegesis paper, take a look at several commentaries on the same passage. This exercise will likely reveal how even scholars disagree with one another on the meaning of a text.

2. Read Psalm 1. Compose a brief outline of this psalm and then analyze the text according to your outline. In your analysis consider especially the main point of each section, the images and their function, and the overall meaning of the psalm in light of these parts.

3. Read carefully Luke 2:1–21. (1) Divide the story into scenes. What is the action in each scene? (2) Identify and note briefly the significance of each of the following aspects of the text: date; location (city, "manger"); characters (human and non-human); reactions of the characters to the birth; the content of the angels' message. (3) What is the theme of this story? What is the tone? Is there any irony in the story? How do the scenes you identified work together to produce a complete narrative? (4) Does the story hint at any themes or conflicts that you might expect to find in the remainder of the book of Luke?

4. Reread Psalm 19. Make a list of about ten to fifteen key words, phrases, or images whose significance you would need to explore and explain if you chose to write a paper on this psalm.

5. Review chapter 11, section 6, pp. 172–87, "Resources for Detailed Analysis."

6. Read carefully the sections of detailed analysis in the sample exegesis papers in Appendixes C and D.

CHAPTER SEVEN

Synthesis
THE FIFTH ELEMENT

We shall not cease from exploration,
And the end of all our exploring
Will be to arrive where we started
And know the place for the first time.
—*T. S. Eliot,* Four Quartets

"What is the punch line?"—*J. Christiaan Beker*[1]

What is the main point, or what are the main points, of the text?

In analyzing the details of the text with the greatest amount of care and precision possible, you have been dealing with the proverbial trees rather than the forest. After doing so, however, you must now turn to the forest and attempt to see what the trees look like as a whole. To return to another metaphor we have used, it is time to look at the big picture, at the puzzle as a whole.

Making a Synthesis of the Text

To synthesize is to pull various elements together into some kind of unified whole. Synthesizing, then, is a disciplined

---

[1] Asked of every text and in every class by this late professor at Princeton Theological Seminary.

but creative act of integration. In making a synthesis of the passage, you are bringing together all that you have thought or said so far. You are not, however, simply making a summary; you are drawing a conclusion about the text's essential meaning, about its purpose or function, as you have come to understand it. In literary terms, you are looking to say something about the topic and the theme of the text—both its subject matter and its slant or perspective on that subject. Harking back to your original guesswork, you are now turning your guesswork and careful analysis into a coherent reading of the text as a whole.

As you attempt to synthesize your findings, ask yourself questions like these:

- What is the main point of each part of the text, and how do the parts make a whole? Can the main point be located accurately in one word, phrase, image, or verse, or does it come only from the content and/or structure of the text as a whole?

- Why do you think the passage was included in this biblical book? What might have been the purpose(s) or function(s) of the text for its original authors and readers?

- What claims did the text make upon its original hearers or readers? What response might the author have desired from the readers? What effects—intentional or not—might the text have had on its first hearers or readers?

As you ask yourself these questions, never forget that you are reading religious literature; the authors and their texts are making religious claims that are intended not merely to inform but also to transform their readers.

The search for a "main point" does not begin at the end of the exegesis or at the end of the paper. It is part of the process, part of the hermeneutical circle, as you look at the parts and the whole, the whole and the parts. Nevertheless, as you approach the conclusion of your work on the text, you may wish to look back again at the contexts, structure, and details of the text with the specific purpose of formulating your understanding of the main point of the text. Some specific questions to ask—which may already have been asked of the text—include:

- Is there any repetition of words, ideas, or images that might indicate not only the structure but also the theme of the text? Is there a governing idea or metaphor? a central motif?

- Does the structure of the text indicate its focus? Is there a center point? inclusio? contrast?

- Does the beginning or the end of the text reveal its main concern?

- Are there significant relationships among the various components of the text that might indicate the overall rhetorical purpose of the text?

After considering the questions suggested above, state your conclusions clearly and creatively. That is, do not merely repeat what you have already said in the detailed analysis or in the introduction, but describe in a new way what the passage is all about.

Although detailed analysis is very important, one's synthesis of the passage is an important indication of the fruits of the exegetical process. No reader of the biblical text should be in the position of being unable to "see the forest for the trees." For those who read the Bible as sacred literature, this step of synthesis is extraordinarily crucial, since the task of theological reflection will be heavily influenced by the reader's overall understanding of the passage.

Ambiguity and Polyvalence

It is sometimes the hope of well-meaning students of the Bible that careful exegesis, attention to all the details, will produce a definitive interpretation of the text. Perusing several commentaries or articles on a particular Bible passage ought to defuse this understandable but erroneous hope. Despite—or even because of—careful investigation of every detail of the text, a good exegete may conclude that this or that aspect of the text, or even the text as a whole, is ambiguous, or uncertain, as to its meaning. In some cases, the ambiguity will be due to insufficient knowledge of the historical and cultural situation in which the text was produced. In other cases, it will be due to insufficient knowledge of the vocabulary or grammar used in the text or to unclear arrangements of words, phrases, or sentences.

Ambiguity, however, is not always in the eye of the beholder. It is not always the "fault" of the reader. Sometimes the text itself is inherently ambiguous; we would probably conclude that the author intended it to be that way. Deliberate ambiguity is evocative, allowing or even forcing readers to ponder the text more carefully, asking "What in the world does this mean?" Ambiguity can be an invitation to engagement. Readers of John's Gospel will recall that Jesus' ambiguous statement "You must be born anew" or "from above" (John 3:3, 7) prompted one of that Gospel's most significant exchanges.

Ambiguity, whether intentional or not, also allows for various interpretations of a text, all of which—if arrived at responsibly—have some claim to validity. In fact, since there is ambiguity in every historical reconstruction and every literary analysis, and since exegesis is more like an art than a science, we should expect a text to mean different things to different people, even if those people employ the same basic methods of analyzing the text. The process of exegesis brings together a text, a set of contexts in which the text is located, and a reader located in yet another context. The results of this process are bound to vary. In fact, my own careful reading of a text this year and next may be quite different. This is because every biblical text is so richly multidimensional, and its readers and their contexts so richly varied, that we should speak of the meanings—plural—of a text rather than the meaning—singular.[2] For those who hear in and through the Bible the voice of God, this does not mean that God is fickle but that God's

---

[2] Some interpreters prefer to speak of a text's singular meaning and its multiple applications. Even if this understanding of meaning were theoretically correct, it would not functionally alter the way in which we seek and discover the rich multiplicity of dimensions of meaning that any text bears.

voice is not only constant and faithful but also fresh, new, and creative.

This is not to say that a text imposes no limits on our interpretation of it or that a text can mean anything we want it to mean. It does mean, however, that a text has multiple legitimate readings, both in terms of its original meaning in context and in terms of its abiding significance.

An example may serve to illustrate this point. The image of a "city on a hill" from Matthew 5:14 has a long history of interpretation, much of it within American religious and especially political contexts. A careful reading of the text in context is quite provocative. There are echoes of Isaiah 2, which declares that the nations shall ascend to Jerusalem (Zion) and live in peace at some future date. This intertextuality suggests Israel's—or a renewed Israel's —eschatological witness to the Gentiles. The image of city lights on a hill would be vivid to residents of both Judea and Galilee. The nature of this light as "good works" (Matthew 5:16) gives focus, though not specificity, to the manner of the witness. Every image points to the exemplary mission of a community, specifically Israel or the early disciples and church as the continuation of Israel.

The Christian church legitimately inherits that image and applies it to itself in various times and ways. Thus "community" and "good works," the text's two dominant images, have been subject to a variety of legitimate readings. However, the application of these images to a nonreligious entity (e.g., the United States) for its nonreligious deeds (e.g., political freedom, democracy, etc.) stretches the limit of interpretation to the breaking point. Some readings, it has been said, do violence to the text. There must be some limits to what the text can mean.

To use an old analogy, a text is like a diamond with many facets, none of which is fully seen by any one observer. We may refer to this phenomenon as the *polyvalence* of a text. Polyvalence is the condition of possessing multiple senses. More precisely, since a text does impose some restrictions on our interpretation, we should speak of its *limited* polyvalence.[3] As each of us attempts to synthesize the various details in the text that we have observed and analyzed, the different minor conclusions to which various readers have arrived begin to add up, and the "grand total"—the understanding of the text as a whole—may be much more than the sum of the various parts.

★ Chapter Summary

- Synthesizing is not merely summarizing but rather a creative act of drawing a conclusion about the meaning and function of the text.

- Several features of a text may provide hints as to its essential topic and theme.

- For various reasons, including the inherent character of the text itself, the meaning of a text may be ambiguous.

- Because exegesis is an art (a craft) as well as a science (a technique), and because every biblical text is multifaceted, a text has a variety of legitimate readings; it possesses limited, though not infinite, polyvalence.

↖ Practical Hints

1. Keep a record of the possible key point(s) as you work through the exegetical process, but save your formulation of the synthesis until you have time to step back and look at all your details holistically.

2. When you have a sense for the text as a whole, write it down in one good (even if complex) sentence, trying to use the key terms or images of the text itself as much as possible while also analyzing the interrelationship of the way the key parts constitute the whole.

---

[3] I am less comfortable with the evocative term "restricted infinity"—though I understand its appeal. See Tate, *Biblical Interpretation,* 211.

👁 For Further Insight and Practice

1. Reread Psalm 19. In one well-written sentence, state your understanding of the meaning of this psalm, making sure to include the results of your outline work from your earlier study of it.

2. Read the story about the prophet Elijah, King Ahab, and the prophets of Baal in 1 Kings 18:1–40. What are the chief religious claims being made in and through this story? What political and social functions would this text have had when it was first told or written? Why might the compiler of 1 Kings have preserved this story for future readers?

3. Read the collection of short stories in Luke 8:22–56. How are these stories related to one another? What seems to be the main point of each and the point of the collection as a whole?

4. Read carefully Romans 8:28–39 and make a brief outline of the text. Then state, in one or two sentences, the main point of the text as you understand it.

5. Review chapter 11, section 7, pp. 187–88, "Resources for Synthesis."

6. Carefully read the sections on synthesis in the sample exegesis papers in the back of this book, Appendixes C and D.

CHAPTER EIGHT

Reflection

THE SIXTH ELEMENT

The Text Today

"Search the Scriptures, not as though thou
wouldst make a concordance but an application."
—*John Donne*

"Apply yourself wholly to the text;
apply the text wholly to yourself."
—*Johann Albrecht Bengel*

***What does this text mean for readers other
than the original ones?***

***What does it mean to you? What does it
mean to your faith community?***

Reflection on a biblical text hardly begins at the end. The
exegetical process is, of course, a process of reflection from
start to finish. After careful analysis and synthesis have
occurred, however, you are in a better position to think
carefully and systematically about the significance of the
text. At this point, the primary question shifts from "What?"
to "So what?"

This stage of exegesis, though avoided by some readers, is
really a natural final element in the process. Great works of
art (including religious literature) inescapably invite engagement. They have an inherent capacity to inspire the
imagination and to create new possibilities for thinking and
living. The ultimate goal of exegesis—of "leading out" from

the text—is to consider carefully the text's invitation to the imagination, to the spirit. In this chapter we look at some possible goals in and methods for such reflection on the text.

Five Interpretive Postures

People reflect on and respond to biblical texts, I would suggest, from one of five basic perspectives, or "interpretive postures."[1] The technical term for such a basic interpretive perspective or posture is "hermeneutic," a word derived from the name of the Greek god Hermes (the Roman god Mercury), the messenger or interpreter of the other gods. Each of these groups of readers looks for, and finds, something different in the biblical texts. Each hermeneutic has a legitimate role in the ongoing interpretation of the Bible as a literary classic of the human spirit and has something to contribute to the other hermeneutical readings. These postures are more or less appropriate, of course, for believing individuals and communities. Indeed, it is difficult to imagine believers being able to sustain themselves as a community for long without a basic hermeneutic of consent or trust toward their sacred texts.

A HERMENEUTIC OF ANTIPATHY

A hermeneutic of antipathy (opposition) is the perspective held by those who find the Bible itself, or its effects, to be dangerous to human freedom, the quest for truth, or some other cherished ideal. Those who approach the Bible from this point of view are apt not only to be critical of the "premodern" world view of the texts but also of what they perceive as the (un)ethical consequences of living according to its values: violence and war, intolerance and hatred, and so on. A typical question from this perspective might be, "What erroneous view of the world and what

---

[1] Tate, *Biblical Interpretation,* 167, uses the term "interpretive framework."

deleterious consequences for human life together does this text perpetuate?"

A HERMENEUTIC OF APPRECIATION OR NONCOMMITMENT

A hermeneutic of appreciation or noncommitment is the perspective held by those whose primary interest in the biblical text is not religious but literary or historical. They have no prior antipathy to the text nor any prior commitment to the text as an inspired or authoritative document—though they may find part or all of it either disturbing or inspiring. They read the Bible with at least as much seriousness as they read, say, Aristotle or Shakespeare. Sometimes, in fact, such interpreters read the Bible more carefully and creatively than those who are steeped in a tradition or community that formally takes the Bible to be its authoritative guide but is unable to read the text in new and different ways. A typical question that a person operating with a hermeneutic of appreciation or noncommitment might ask is, "What does this text tell me about the human quest for meaning in life, and to what degree do I, or do I not, resonate with its point of view?"

A HERMENEUTIC OF DISCERNMENT OR INQUIRY

A hermeneutic of discernment or inquiry is the point of view held by those who have neither rejected nor avoided a formal commitment to hearing the Bible as sacred text, nor made such a commitment. They are "looking for answers," and the Bible is one place (perhaps one of many places) in which they are seeking perspective for life. A typical question from this point of view might be, "What mode of life does this text suggest, and how satisfying is its suggestion—intellectually, spiritually, ethically—compared to others with which I am wrestling?"

A HERMENEUTIC OF SUSPICION

A hermeneutic of suspicion is typically employed by those who have been part of a religious community or tradition and who have reacted against what they perceive to be the

misuse of the Bible as a source of religious authority by traditions and communities (their own and/or others). The
suspicion may be directed against readings that are believed
to neglect the historical contexts and conditioning of the
Bible or, more often today, against readings that have been
used, they believe, to marginalize or oppress minorities.
The oppressed may include the poor, women, African
Americans, Jews, gays and lesbians, or other groups not
within the mainstream of society or of the interpretive tradition. Those who embrace a hermeneutic of suspicion believe that the interpretive tradition and (usually) the text
itself are subject to criticism and even potentially dangerous. A typical question that a person operating with a hermeneutic of suspicion might ask is, "Is there some way to
rescue this text from its oppressive perspective and use so
that it can liberate the very people that it was written to
oppress or the people who have been oppressed by later
interpretations?"

A HERMENEUTIC OF CONSENT OR TRUST

A hermeneutic of consent or trust is the interpretive framework within which most practicing Jews and Christians read
the Bible. They give the Bible the "benefit of the doubt"
and conclude that because the people of God known as Jews
and Christians have heard "the word of the Lord" in the
Bible for thousands of years, they also may still hear from
God through this book. Those who have examined other
hermeneutics and found them either unwarranted or inappropriate as their fundamental interpretive posture often
still attempt to take them seriously. Their decision to give
the Bible the "benefit of the doubt" as a source of religious
authority is not made easily and should not be interpreted
as either simplistic, antiquated, or anti-intellectual. They
may, in fact, share some of the concerns of those who read
suspiciously. A typical question that a person operating with
a hermeneutic of consent or trust might ask is, "What is the
word of God for us in this text?" or "How do we see the situation of God's people addressed in the text analogous to

our situation today, and what is our appropriate response of faith and life to this word?"

The Two Horizons

Readers with a hermeneutic of either suspicion or trust are deliberately reading the Bible with an eye on the "two horizons" mentioned in chapter 1 of this book. They want to know the meaning of the text in its original context as well as the possible significance of the text in their own contemporary context.[2]

As noted earlier, some scholars therefore distinguish between exegesis and reflection, between textual *meaning* and textual (contemporary) *significance,* between "what it meant" and "what it means."[3] For methodological, pedagogical, or organizational purposes, these distinctions may be fine. If we understand exegesis, however, as reading the text in its contexts, there is no inherent reason to bifurcate the reading process so completely. To be sure, exegesis is concerned first of all with the meaning of the text in its *original* contexts, but if a sacred text is worth its salt as *sacred* text, or even as *artistic* text, then (1) it must make some ongoing claims on its contemporary audience, and (2) those claims must have some connection to the claims made on its original audience. Furthermore, admitting that we have an interest in the meaning of the text—since exegesis without

---

[2]One could also argue that a hermeneutic of discernment or appreciation and even of antipathy also involves the two horizons, since readers within these hermeneutical postures may be interested in (or interested in opposing) the text in the contemporary setting. However, readers within these hermeneutical postures differ from those in the other two by not being part of a community of interpretation that is committed by its very nature to the two horizons.

[3]This distinction was carefully formulated by Krister Stendahl in, for example, "Biblical Theology, Contemporary" in *Interpreter's Dictionary of the Bible* (ed. G. A. Buttrick; 4 vols.; Nashville: Abingdon, 1962), 1:418–32.

presuppositions is impossible—keeps us honest with ourselves and with one another so that we are less likely to
engage in *eisegesis* (reading into the text) in the name of
objectivity.

The notion of "two horizons" is built on the theory of interpretation that claims that we cannot truly read, interpret, or
understand a text until we engage it, until we somehow fuse
its "horizon" with our own. According to theorists like
Hans-Georg Gadamer and Paul Ricoeur, the reading or
interpretive process is incomplete until or unless that fusion
occurs. The process of considering the two horizons is sometimes called "application" (Gadamer) or "appropriation"
(Ricoeur).[4] For believers, this application or appropriation
can never be merely intellectual or theoretical. The final
goal of exegesis, as we will see below, is actualization or
embodiment—living the text. To put it more sharply, the
ultimate goal of exegesis is for the individual and community to become a *living exegesis* of the text.

The notion of the "two horizons" is built also on the principle of analogy. The contemporary reader of the text
attempts to discern the message of the text not only in its
original setting but also in possible analogous situations
today—similarly, yet differently, since all analogies have
both similarity and difference built into them. Moreover,
when the Bible is read as a word from God, readers must
always be prepared to have their horizons enlarged and
to have new horizons created.[5] We cannot, therefore, under-
estimate the importance of imagination—though disciplined
(and, one might say, Spirit-guided), rather than freewheel-

---

[4] The complex theoretical work of these two philosophers may
be found in Hans-Georg Gadamer, *Truth and Method* (trans. Joel
Weinsheimer and Donald G. Marshall; 2d rev. ed.; New York:
Crossroad, 1989); Paul Ricoeur, *Interpretation Theory: Discourse and
the Surplus of Meaning* (Fort Worth, Tex.: Texas Christian University
Press, 1976); and idem, *Hermeneutics and the Human Sciences* (ed.
John B. Thompson; Cambridge: Cambridge University Press, 1981).

[5] This is a major thesis of Thiselton, *New Horizons in Hermeneutics,* summarized on 619.

ing imagination—in the interpretation of the Bible for our own contexts.

Some basic hints for reflecting on the text are offered in the next section. But perhaps the most crucial point to remember in this process of reflection is to avoid dullness, which occurs when readers engage in what Anthony Thiselton calls "premature assimilation." Premature assimilation takes place when readers jump into the application of a text without sufficient thought and without respect for the distance between the two horizons, between then and now. The result, says Thiselton, is that "interaction between the two horizons of the texts and readers will . . . appear *uneventful, bland, routine, and entirely unremarkable.*"[6] Furthermore, premature assimilation will result in our controlling or domesticating the text rather than allowing the text to challenge us.

Some Ways to Think about "The Two Horizons"

Now that you have carefully reflected on the meaning of the text in its original contexts, you can intelligently think about its broader, deeper, or ongoing meaning. First of all, paraphrase the central meaning of the text; that is, put it in your own words.

Have you heard or read this passage before? In what context? Is this passage similar to, or different from, other Bible passages you know? Do you know what place this text has had in the life of Jews and/or Christians? in history generally?

What universal hopes, fears, beliefs, and values do you see expressed in this text? What unique or unusual beliefs and values? What does this text claim about God, human beings, and the relationship between God and people? Specifically, what does this text affirm about:

- God

- Persons specially related to God

---

[6] Ibid., 8 (emphasis his).

- Other supernatural beings

- Divine or sacred history

- Human redemption by God

- Human commitment to God

- Community

- Ethics/daily life[7]

How do *you* react to this text? Do you like it? Why or why not? What emotions does it stir up in you? Joy? Wonder? Anger? Frustration? Fear? What response do you have to the image or actions of God implicit in this passage?

Does this text challenge you in any way? Does it open up any new horizons of understanding and insight? Do you feel differently about the passage after careful study than you did on first reading it? How does your own religious and social location affect your understanding of and reaction to the text? How might you feel about this text if you were part of a different time, place, race, socio-economic group, or religious community?

Do you see any contemporary issues or situations that seem similar, or analogous, to the issues or situations addressed in or by the biblical text? How are they similar? dissimilar?

In a word, what claims about God, and about God's claim on us, does the text make? Are these central, marginal, or antithetical to the understanding of God and God's claim on us that you, your religious tradition, or others you know have? If there is conflict between the text and your perspective, how might you resolve that conflict? Will you

- ignore the text?

- challenge the text?

- look for a means of reconciliation?

- review and revise your exegesis?

---

[7] List adapted from Robbins, *Exploring the Texture of Texts*, 120–31.

- alter your beliefs and/or behavior?

- consult with others?

These are all possible (and frequently practiced) options.

As noted in the previous chapter, we should never be surprised when people find different meanings in the same biblical text; even professional exegetes disagree about the original meaning of the text, so why would we expect anything less in reflecting on its contemporary significance? This does not mean that the text is simply like a ventriloquist's dummy to express the capricious desires of the interpreter.[8] What matters for all interpreters is that each interpreter be able to ground his or her reflection in a careful analysis of the text and to engage both the text and others in a spirit of humility.

After thinking through all these things, then, ask yourself finally, What might be the significance, if any, of this text for today? If readers took the message of this text seriously, how would their lives be different?

LIVING EXEGESIS

To raise this last question—if readers took the message of this text seriously, how would their lives be different?—is to raise the ultimate question of exegesis. It is to answer the text's own invitation to engage the text on its own terms— as imagination-transforming and life-transforming word. Readers who decline to respond to this invitation are not thereby rendered bad or unwelcome readers, but they have, in some sense, truncated the reading process.

Among persons and communities of faith this invitation is normally taken seriously. It is the question of "embodiment" or "actualization." We might also refer to this final element of exegesis, as noted above, as "living exegesis." The goal of this "method" is for the exegete, whether an individual or a community, in some sense to become the

---

[8]This wonderful image is from Schneiders, *The Revelatory Text*, xxxi.

text it reads. This "becoming the text" does not mean a wholesale replication of all the cultural values and other dimensions of the text. Rather, it means a discerning engagement with the text from within the particular interpretive posture of the reader(s). In narrative terms, the community or individual as exegete continues the narrative of the text by being part of its ongoing embodiment in the world, a kind of narrative embodiment. This is sometimes referred to as "performing" the text of Scripture.[9] This performance may also be an expression of what many have called for in theology and life: "creative fidelity."

This final task of exegesis raises two fundamental questions, two questions that—appropriately—constitute a hermeneutical circle of their own:

- What kind of community does this text urge its readers to embody?

- What kind of community is required to hear this text as invitation and to embody it with "creative fidelity"?

These questions can be asked and answered by any astute readers. For those who hear in the Bible a word from God, however, asking and answering such questions is not merely a possibility but a divine imperative.

The notion of "living exegesis" or narrative embodiment does not mean the uncritical acceptance and wooden replication of every aspect of every text. (Even murder is narrated in biblical texts!) Rather, living exegesis requires imaginative reflection on the text in light of the convictions inherent in the hermeneutical stance adopted by the readers and the traditions of their communities.

On occasion, therefore, even the faithful religious individual or community finds texts in the Bible that seem to contradict their fundamental convictions. An example might be Psalm 137, which describes "bashing the Babylonian babies' brains on the boulders," as someone once put it.

---

[9] See, among others, Nicholas Lash, "Performing Scripture," in *Theology on the Way to Emmaus* (London: SCM, 1986), 37–46.

When encountering such texts, the faithful have traditionally responded with pragmatic exegetical moves such as allegorical interpretation or reinterpretation in light of later texts and contexts. In so doing, readers create what we might call counter-readings of the text. In these cases, the community then embodies a living counter-exegesis of the text as its members seek to discern a meaning in and out of the text that is consistent with their most fundamental convictions. For example, Christian readers of Psalm 137 would normally appeal finally to the teaching and example of Jesus regarding enemy-love to provide a fully canonical exegesis (and thus a counter-exegesis) of Psalm 137.

This approach can, of course, be taken to an extreme. It cannot, however, be avoided, at least on occasion. For people of faith, the imperative to read the text as word of God may require a basic posture of trust, but it also requires an openness to difficult questions and new perspectives when problematic texts are taken seriously.

★ Chapter Summary

- There are five basic interpretive postures or hermeneutics: antipathy, appreciation or noncommitment, discernment or inquiry, suspicion, and consent or trust.

- Consideration of the two horizons of past and present—reflection and application or appropriation—is an essential element of a complete reading process, but the application must not be done carelessly or prematurely.

- It is important to ask the right questions of a text when considering its broader, deeper, or ongoing meaning.

- For people of faith, the essential question is, "What claims about God and about God's claims on us does the text make?"

- People of faith seek to embody or become a living exegesis of the text. This is done creatively and sometimes even critically.

Practical Hints

1. Since reflection does not begin at the end of the exegetical process, record preliminary reflections as you work.

2. Try to do at least some of your exegetical research by reading those with clearly theological or other existential interests.

For Further Reflection and Practice

1. Read carefully Psalm 8. State its main point in your own words. What are some contemporary issues to which it might allude? How is the author of this psalm similar to or different from people you know today? What relevance might this psalm have in a technological world?

2. Read the prophetic text in Micah 6:8. Use your imagination to write a short essay on what your community or institution might be like if this text were its motto.

3. Choose a religious, social, or ethical issue of concern. Find at least two biblical passages that might be relevant to your issue. Without doing a detailed exegesis of the texts, write down some initial ideas and questions you have about the use of these texts to address the issue you have chosen.

4. Review chapter 11, section 8, pp. 188–91, "Resources for Reflection."

5. Read the sections of the sample exegesis papers entitled "reflection" in Appendixes C and D. How would you describe and respond to their reflections?

CHAPTER NINE

Expansion and Refinement of the Exegesis

THE SEVENTH ELEMENT

" 'Do you understand what you are reading?' . . .
'How can I, unless someone guides me?' "
—Philip and the Ethiopian eunuch,
Acts 8:30–31 (NRSV)

What tools are available to expand and refine the exegete's work on the text?

What have biblical scholars said about the passage, and how should their work affect yours?

One of the fundamental assumptions of this book is that exegesis can and must be done by the nonspecialist. The student, teacher, or pastor does not need to possess a Ph.D. in biblical studies in order to do excellent exegesis. That assumption does *not* mean, however, that appropriate tools should be neglected or that the work of expert guides should be ignored. The "tools of the trade" and the field of biblical scholarship can and must inform the student's or preacher's own work if that work is to be responsible. Other colleagues in the investigation, partners in the conversation, and artistic instruments are needed.

Tools

Throughout this book reference has been made to a number of tools that are at the disposal of exegetes. When I was in seminary, one of my biblical professors told us that all we really needed (as long as we had mastered the original languages!) was a concordance, a grammar (of Hebrew, Aramaic, or Greek), and a lexicon (dictionary). There is a lot of truth in those words: a good concordance is a tremendous tool, and certain kinds of dictionaries can be helpful.

Most readers, however, will depend on the opinions of scholars working in the original languages. I, for one, am fearful of exegetes who know very little about Hebrew or Greek but do not refrain from making pronouncements based on their limited knowledge. It is still true that a little bit of knowledge is dangerous.

Thus, listed in chapter 11 of this book are numerous tools for biblical study, as well as other sources to consult for additional tools. The careful exegete will make wise use of certain tools without necessarily becoming an expert in ancient languages.

Biblical Scholarship

The published work of scholars can confirm or correct the disciplined discoveries made in the exegetical process as well as resolve unanswered questions that have arisen during the process and generate new ones. Scholars can define unknown terms, show connections to other biblical texts, supply helpful historical information, explain grammatical constructions, and suggest implicit and explicit aspects of the significance of the text.

How many and which scholarly publications should be consulted depends on the nature and purpose of the exegesis. A preacher preparing a Sunday sermon or homily may (or may not) find one or two one-volume commentaries sufficient, whereas a student writing a ten-page exegesis paper will need to consult several detailed commentaries and articles. Some instructors have suggested that a research paper should have about as many items in its working bibliography (the list of works actually used for and cited in the paper) as it has pages of text. That is, for a ten- to twelve-page exegesis paper, one might consult about five to seven commentaries and other books and five to seven articles or chapters in collections of essays. A twenty-page paper might have about twenty items, and so forth. This is only a general guideline, however, and it may not apply to papers shorter than ten pages.

There are some basic starting places that make the search for appropriate resources for an exegesis paper easier.

COMMENTARIES

A good place to begin is with two or three recent major scholarly commentaries covering the passage under consideration. Good commentaries will provide a detailed yet holistic interpretation of the passage in its context. Consulting a variety of commentaries will usually give the reader a variety of readings of particular verses as well as of the text as a whole. Scholarly commentaries will also provide references (in the text, footnotes, or bibliographies) that will suggest relevant commentaries, books, and articles to consult.

Certain commentary series are especially helpful in this regard. For example, the *Word Biblical Commentary, Sacra Pagina,* and *The Anchor Bible* have particularly complete and useful bibliographies for each unit of the text. Other individual commentaries and commentary series also have good bibliographies. At least one of the bibliographies consulted should be less than ten years old; otherwise many of the works listed will be outdated.

BOOKS AND ARTICLES

The next resources to check are some of the standard bibliographical tools for articles and other works published in the field of biblical studies. These tools, which are usually quite comprehensive, may list books or articles that shorter or older bibliographies in commentaries do not contain. The most important of these resources are listed in section 9 of chapter 11. The most efficient way to use the printed bibliographic sources is to scan the volumes published after the latest relevant entry found in the bibliographies consulted within commentaries. For instance, if one of the commentaries includes articles from as late as 1995, searching through indices and abstracts published in 1995 and later will fill in the bibliographic gaps. If you have access to the CD-ROM versions of these tools, you will be able to get a complete list (depending on the specific search you request) of a topic.

Browsing the table of contents of some recent journals (such as those listed in chapter 11, section 6) in the library is also worth doing, especially since printed and electronic indices are never completely up to date. Finding one or two current articles on a topic or passage will usually lead to additional books and articles on the subject of the exegetical paper. (While the success of this effort is largely a matter of serendipity and should therefore not consume a lot of time and energy, it frequently pays off.) References to an older book or article in several recent sources normally indicate the enduring importance of that older work.

One kind of source that too many exegetes avoid is the work of the great exegetes and preachers of the past—Chrysostom, Augustine, Luther, Wesley, and others. Their literary and theological insights are neglected only to our own detriment. These can be very insightful sources.

Anyone who has ever consulted more than one commentary on a biblical text knows that scholars often disagree on the meaning of a passage. The nonspecialist exegete cannot and should not, therefore, take every sentence from a commentary as "gospel." Rather, each resource must be read carefully and critically, in dialogue with one's own work and with whichever other resources are at hand. One's own work may be just as valid as that of a commentator. A careful interpretation of the text, challenged, informed, and refined by the work of scholars, is the goal of this step in the exegetical process.

★ Chapter Summary

- People who do good exegesis will consult the tools and resources compiled by experts.

- Pursuing scholarly contributions is made possible through notes and bibliographies in various resources and through several kinds of bibliographical tools.

↖ Practical Hints

1. Professors and advanced students may be able to give guidance about general or particular resources. Students may wish to begin their research with a brief conversation, for example, with their professor. For the most part, however, exegetes should rely on standard bibliographies, books, and indices, such as those listed in chapter 11, section 9, to point them in the right direction. When this method produces questions, it is time again to consult with the experts if possible.

2. The wide divergence of opinion in biblical interpretation can be unsettling. The best thing to do is to attempt to organize diversity into various major options and then to weigh for yourself the merits of each option as presented by the proponents of that view. Some articles and commentaries helpfully set out the major interpretations of a particular issue (such as the meaning of a word, the purpose or date of a document, etc.) as well as the strengths and weaknesses of each point of view; these are very valuable pages to find on a controversial issue.

3. As for the amount of information, this too can be overwhelming. Feeling besieged by data is a normal response. The key is to realize that you may be able to gather helpful facts or interpretations from every responsible resource and perspective that you read, even if you disagree with the exegete's overall interpretation. Whatever you read, look for the main pieces of information or perspectives, record them, and begin to evaluate them. Are the arguments valid or questionable? strong or weak? Are the facts and perspectives that are offered *central* to the understanding of the text? *valuable? dubious? extraneous?* Use these questions to decide what matters for the interpretation of the text and to decide what to exclude and include in the writing of your paper.

👁 For Further Insight and Practice

1. Consult at least two scholarly commentaries on Psalm 1. Write up the results of your research and indicate any differences between what you learned and what you thought about the passage based on your previous reading of this psalm.

2. Read at least two scholarly commentaries on Matthew 16:18. List the various major interpretations of this text, your view of the strengths and weaknesses of each, and the reasons for the interpretation that you find most compelling.

3. Recall your earlier analysis of the outline and main point of Romans 8:28–39. Compare this to the comments of at least two scholarly commentaries.

4. Construct a bibliography of articles and essays on Isaiah 6 written in the last decade.

5. Review chapter 11, section 9, pp. 191–93, "Bibliographic Resources," and chapter 11 as a whole to familiarize or refamiliarize yourself with the various resources at your disposal.

CHAPTER TEN

Exegesis and the Exegete

ERRORS TO AVOID, DISCOVERIES TO MAKE

"[H]owever a particular epoch or a particular
community may define a proper mode of attention or a licit area of interest, there will always be
something else and something different to say."
—*Frank Kermode*[1]

You have now worked through the seven elements that
make up the process of exegesis—carefully reading and analyzing a biblical text—that is advocated in this book. You
are now ready to choose a passage to study and analyze in
detail. First, however, some final words of both caution and
encouragement.

Two general common errors in using this method of exegesis can easily be avoided if they are known in advance. First,
some students become so completely attached to the procedure that they lose any sense of original thinking or creativity. The purpose of the method is not to stifle creativity
but to provide a means of *disciplined investigation and imagination.* Students and teachers must always be engaged in
asking new questions of the texts and of themselves.

Second, when writing exegesis papers, some students find
this method to be repetitious. The introduction, outline,
analysis, synthesis, and even their own reflections sound

---

[1] Frank Kermode, *Forms of Attention* (Chicago: University of
Chicago Press, 1985), 62.

much the same. This problem can be avoided in part by keeping one's observations succinct and by constantly looking for what is hidden and unique in the text, rather than what is obvious and common. Moreover, each section of the paper should carry the interpretation of the passage a step further; each part should move the reader's understanding to a new level, not just repeat earlier observations and conclusions.

In addition to these general mistakes to avoid, there are several common mistakes students make at each stage of the exegetical process when writing papers. The following suggestions, each of which echoes one of the practical hints that appears in the appropriate chapter, are offered based on my experience with many hundreds of exegetical papers:

The Task

Do not attempt to execute methods that are beyond your ability. Do not attempt, say, to do tradition criticism without the necessary skills or to discuss the intricacies of Hebrew grammar and vocabulary on the basis of an interlinear Bible. Rather, play to your strengths. Develop and use the skills any careful reader needs to have: observing, questioning, making connections, recognizing patterns, and so on. These will take you a long way.

The Text

Do not choose a passage if you are unwilling to learn about it and from it, even to have your basic presuppositions about its meaning challenged. Therefore, it is probably best not to choose a passage that is *so* emotionally difficult for you, for whatever reason, that your paper becomes more of an exegesis of your psychological state or personal history than of the text itself. Rather, choose a text that is of interest to you and that you will attempt to engage honestly, but consider avoiding one that is so problematic for you that your work will be an exercise in futility. (This advice may sound unnecessary or even unscholarly. While I certainly do not advocate fear of discovery and challenge, I recognize, from many years of experience, that there are occasions in which choosing to do an exegesis paper—with the pressure of academic requirements and evaluation—on a difficult passage is not the best way to reckon with that passage. My concerns are not primarily academic, nor theological or "doctrinal," but personal and even pastoral.)

Element 1—Introduction (Survey)

Do not yield to the temptation to provide an extended synopsis of every part of your paper in the introduction; otherwise it will be too long, and the other sections will become repetitious. Rather, use the introduction to hook the reader and provide a succinct overview of the paper, with primary attention to the flow (parts) of the paper and to your thesis.

Element 2—Contextual Analysis

Historical Context. Do not think of your paper as a mini-encyclopedia that reports to the reader every imaginable fact about the time period or community that produced, or is addressed in, your text. Rather, provide a general overview as needed, but focus on the particular aspects of the historical, social, and cultural contexts that are directly relevant to your specific text.

Literary Context. Do not discuss your passage per se in this section at all. Rather, this is the place to analyze the place of your passage in the larger whole. This may include a discussion of the outline and flow of the book in order to situate your text within the larger work, but do not construct an outline of your particular passage here. Discussion of the structure and movement of the passage itself belongs in the section on formal analysis.

Element 3—Formal Analysis (Form, Structure, and Movement)

Do not turn this section into a discussion of the biblical book in which your text is found. The focus of this section of the paper is on the form, structure, and movement of *your particular passage,* not of the biblical book. Some discussion of the genre of the book may be appropriate, but even here the focus is on how the nature of that genre affects the interpretation of your passage. Do not provide an extended discussion of the characteristics of psalms or gospels or letters in general. Also, do not provide an outline of the book, but rather an outline of the passage itself. If a brief summary and/or outline of the entire book is included in the paper, it should appear in the section on literary context, not this section.

Element 4—Detailed Analysis

Do not allow the first sections of your paper to monopolize your space, leaving you insufficient room truly for detailed analysis. Rather, plan your paper carefully so that you devote at least 50 percent of the paper to detailed analysis.

Element 5—Synthesis

Do not try to restate everything you have said in your paper. Rather, restate your thesis, now that you have demonstrated it, creatively pulling together the most important results of all that you have unveiled and argued in the course of the paper. This will indicate to the reader what you take to be the essential significance of the text.

Element 6—Reflection

Do not use this occasion to prepare a sermon on the text, unless specifically asked to do so. Rather, this space provides you the opportunity to be suggestive, even open-ended, in your remarks. The best reflections are often very subtle; they are seldom hammerlike.

Element 7—Expansion and Refinement of the Exegesis

Do not make this a separate part of the paper as a whole or of each section of the paper. Rather, although this is a separate step in the process, done after your own initial exegesis, the results of your research are integrated into the paper as a whole. The result is a paper in which your own thesis and interpretation drive the essay, but in which you interact with and gain support from others, who are your conversation partners.

A superior exegesis sheds unique light on a biblical text because the exegesis is the result of one's own personal engagement with the text. Such an exegesis is really an expression of the unique intersection of contexts—those of the author, the original readers, and the interpreter. If you apply yourself to the study of the Bible, always keeping an eye on its various contexts—as well as your own—you may well be surprised at what you discover.

CHAPTER ELEVEN

Resources for Exegesis

"But above all, I beg and entreat your clemency
earnestly to intercede with the lord commissary,
that he would deign to allow me the use of
my Hebrew Bible, Hebrew Grammar, and
Hebrew Lexicon, and that I may employ
my time with that study."
—*William Tyndale, from his prison cell*[1]

"Dictionaries are like watches; the worst is
better than none, and the best cannot be
expected to go quite true."
—*Samuel Johnson*

The following pages contain an annotated bibliography of
scholarly resources to help in the process of exegesis. These
resources are some of the most important and commonly
used tools available for the seventh step, "expansion and
refinement of the exegesis," which is applied to all the other
elements of exegesis. Unlike William Tyndale, however,
many contemporary exegetes do not read, or do not remember, Hebrew and Greek. Thus most of the resources listed
below do not require a knowledge of the original languages,
though in some cases such knowledge helps, and in a few
instances it is absolutely necessary (e.g., to use the Greek NT).

---

[1] Quoted in Frederick W. Danker, *Multipurpose Tools for Bible
Study* (rev. and exp. ed.; Minneapolis: Fortress, 1993), 177.

This part of the book is divided into nine sections, corresponding to the first nine chapters. The resources for chapter 9 are primarily bibliographical tools and other books that point to additional resources. Some resources defy categorization, and many are useful for a variety of steps in the exegetical process. Commentaries, for example, contain not only detailed exegesis but also information about context, about form and structure, and sometimes about the contemporary significance of a text. I have tried to connect these kinds of multi-purpose resources with the element of exegesis for which they are *most* useful.

For a brief list of internet sources, see Appendix E.

I have made no attempt to be exhaustive, only helpful. Serious exegetes will use these works to pursue other resources as needed. And all readers should use whatever resources they discover with appropriate care and caution; all are beneficial, but none is infallible.

In addition to all of the resources listed below, special attention to the following book is in order:

Alexander, Patrick H., et al., eds. *The SBL Handbook of Style.* Peabody, Mass.: Hendrickson, 1999. This unique book, though designed primarily for biblical scholars preparing works for publication, contains a wealth of useful information for students as well as the standards for writing in the biblical field. Students will find the correct usage, spelling, and abbreviations of biblical books and other ancient and modern sources; charts for the transliteration of Hebrew, Aramaic, Greek, and other ancient languages; and both rules for and examples of notes and bibliographical entries. This book is the "Turabian" or MLA style manual for biblical studies.

Section 1. Resources for Understanding the Task

A GENERAL WORK ON READING

Adler, Mortimer J., and Charles Van Doren. *How to Read a Book.* Rev. ed. New York: Simon & Schuster, 1972. A classic on the art of reading and on reading particular kinds of writing.

GENERAL WORKS ON EXEGESIS

This list focuses on books that deal primarily with synchronic and diachronic approaches to the text and those that cover the entire range of approaches. Works primarily on theological or other "existential" approaches to the interpretation of the text are listed under section 8 ("Resources for Reflection") of this part of the book.

Coggins, R. J., and J. L. Houlden. *A Dictionary of Biblical Interpretation.* Philadelphia: Trinity, 1990. A handy, concise, and insightful set of short entries and longer essays on terms, methods, and people.

Gillingham, Susan E. *One Bible, Many Voices: Different Approaches to Biblical Studies.* Grand Rapids: Eerdmans, 1998. An introductory text on the "plurality" involved in both the making and the reading of the Bible, arguing for a theological approach integrated with historical-critical and literary approaches. Illustrated with specific reference to the Psalms in general and to Psalm 8 in particular.

Hayes, John H., gen. ed. *Dictionary of Biblical Interpretation.* 2 vols. Nashville: Abingdon, 1999. Contains articles on significant theories of interpretation, approaches, methods, and key practitioners, both past and present.

Hayes, John H., and Carl R. Holladay. *Biblical Exegesis: A Beginner's Handbook.* Rev. ed. Atlanta: John Knox, 1987. The revision of an excellent standard treatment of exegetical methods, largely in the historical-critical tradition but with attention to literary approaches, for the beginning and intermediate student. A good next-read.

Kaiser, Otto, and Werner G. Kümmel. *Exegetical Method: A Student's Handbook.* Translated by E. V. N. Goetschius and M. J. O'Connell. Rev. ed. New York: Seabury, 1981. The English translation of a standard German introduction to historical-critical exegesis written for beginning students, with sections on the OT and the NT.

Krentz, Edgar. *The Historical-Critical Method.* Guides to Biblical Scholarship. Philadelphia: Fortress, 1975. A short, classic treatment of the diachronic approach with respect to its origins and uses.

Longman, Tremper, III. *Literary Approaches to Biblical Interpretation.* Grand Rapids: Zondervan, 1987. A very good introduction to the theory and application of literary approaches, with a historical survey, evaluations of methods, and sample analyses of both prose and poetry in the Bible (especially the OT).

McKenzie, Steven L., and Stephen R. Haynes, eds. *To Each Its Own Meaning: An Introduction to Biblical Criticisms and Their Application.* Rev. and expanded. Louisville: Westminster John Knox, 1999. A superb, very readable collection of essays on various diachronic, synchronic, literary, and ideological methods under the headings "traditional methods of biblical criticism," "expanding the tradition," and "overturning the tradition." Each chapter discusses and illustrates the method and provides a bibliography. An excellent next-read after this book.

Montague, George T. *Understanding the Bible: A Basic Introduction to Biblical Interpretation.* New York: Paulist, 1997. A helpful, engaging history of biblical interpretation and its various approaches from the ancient church to the end of the twentieth century, from a Catholic perspective but of ecumenical interest.

Robbins, Vernon K. *Exploring the Texture of Texts: A Guide to Socio-Rhetorical Interpretation.* Valley Forge, Pa.: Trinity, 1996. An excellent, detailed introduction to socio-rhetorical criticism as a broad, integrated approach to interpretation that includes analysis of a text's five dimensions or "textures": inner texture, intertexture, social and cultural texture, ideological texture, and sacred (theological) texture. Although the focus of the book and the examples are drawn largely from the Gospels, the principles apply to the exegesis of any text.

Ryken, Leland. *Words of Delight: A Literary Introduction to the Bible.* 2d ed. Grand Rapids: Baker, 1992. A superb introduction to traditional literary criticism as applied to the Bible, covering the elements of biblical narrative, poetry, and other forms in both Testaments. Full of short readings of specific texts.

Soulen, R. N. *Handbook of Biblical Criticism.* 2d ed. Atlanta: John Knox, 1981. Although a bit dated, a helpful dictionary-like handbook of terms.

Tate, W. Randolph. *Biblical Interpretation: An Integrated Approach.* Rev. ed. Peabody, Mass.: Hendrickson, 1997. For intermediate and perhaps some beginning students, an approach that brings together methods of interpreting the "world behind the text," "the world within the text," and "the world in front of the text." Contains helpful vocabularies, summaries, and bibliographies.

Tiffany, Frederick C., and Sharon H. Ringe. *Biblical Interpretation: A Roadmap.* Nashville: Abingdon, 1996. A basic guide outlining elements of exegesis similar to those proposed in this book, with special emphasis on the effects of social location and the "circular" nature of the process. Contains exegetical examples and a basic bibliography of tools.

Watson, Francis, ed. *The Open Text: New Directions for Biblical Studies.* London: SCM, 1993. A collection of essays corporately and individually offering the thesis that the historical-critical method is insufficient and that a plurality of reading strategies, especially those focused on the reader, is needed.

OLD TESTAMENT EXEGESIS

Barton, John. *Reading the Old Testament: Method in Biblical Study.* Rev. and enlarged. Louisville: Westminster John Knox, 1997. An introduction to and critical analysis of the major criticisms, synchronic and otherwise, arguing for a plurality of approaches and for biblical interpretation as a field in the humanities, not the sciences. For Barton, methods are not rules but descriptive "codifications" of what astute readers have asked and observed about texts. A good next-read for students of the Hebrew Bible/OT.

Exum, J. Cheryl, and David J. A. Clines, eds. *The New Literary Criticism and the Hebrew Bible.* Sheffield: JSOT Press, 1993; Valley Forge, Pa.: Trinity, 1994. A collection of essays from various current literary approaches.

Hens-Piazza, Gina. *Of Methods, Monarchs, and Meanings: A Sociorhetorical Approach to Exegesis.* Macon, Ga.: Mercer University Press, 1996. An approach to OT exegesis that integrates rhetorical criticism (synchronic) and social-science criticism (understood here as a more diachronic approach), with illustrations of the analysis of three texts from 1–2 Samuel and 1 Kings.

House, Paul R., ed. *Beyond Form Criticism: Essays in Old Testament Literary Criticism.* Sources for Biblical and Theological Study 2. Winona Lake, Ind.: Eisenbrauns, 1992. A collection of important previously published essays, introducing and applying various forms of literary and rhetorical criticism of the OT. For intermediate and advanced students.

Moor, Johannes de, ed. *Synchronic or Diachronic: A Debate on Method in Old Testament Exegesis.* Leiden: Brill, 1997. A collection of essays by Dutch and British scholars on diachronic and synchronic approaches and their potential compatibility. For more advanced students.

Steck, Odil Hannes. *Old Testament Exegesis: A Guide to the Methodology.* Translated by James D. Nogalski. 2d ed. SBL Resources for Biblical Study 39. Atlanta: Scholars, 1998. This English edition of a standard, oft-reprinted German text (and approach) is designed for advanced students. After providing an overview of historical-critical work, it treats the general task, method, results, and bibliography for text, literary, transmission-historical, redaction, form, tradition-historical, and historical-setting criticism. The book is full of brief illustrations and contains a helpful bibliography.

Stuart, Douglas. *Old Testament Exegesis: A Primer for Students and Pastors.* Rev. ed. Philadelphia: Westminster, 1984. A basic step-by-step guide that does not demand the use of Hebrew.

Wilson, Robert R. *Sociological Approaches to the Old Testament.* Guides to Biblical Scholarship. Philadelphia: Fortress, 1984.

An early and basic introduction, with application of an "anthropological perspective" to several areas of OT study.

NEW TESTAMENT EXEGESIS

Black, David A., and David S. Dockery. *New Testament Criticism and Interpretation.* Grand Rapids: Zondervan, 1991. A collection of essays for beginning students, from leading evangelical scholars, on interpretive issues and exegetical methods.

Conzelmann, Hans, and Andreas Lindemann. *Interpreting the New Testament: An Introduction to the Principles and Methods of N.T. Exegesis.* Translated by Siegfried S. Schatzmann. Peabody, Mass.: Hendrickson, 1988. A comprehensive handbook, with exercises, to the historical-critical approach to the NT. Also a brief critical introduction to the NT environment and writings. For the advanced student.

Cosby, Michael R. *Portraits of Jesus: An Inductive Approach to the Gospels.* Louisville: Westminster John Knox, 1999. A learning-by-doing approach that has beginning students do close reading of gospel texts to discover literary and theological patterns, themes, and problems.

Egger, Wilhelm. *How to Read the New Testament: An Introduction to Linguistic and Historical-Critical Methodology.* Ed. Hendrikus Boers. Translated by Peter Heinegg. Peabody, Mass.: Hendrickson, 1996. A helpful introduction primarily to the historical-critical approach to the NT.

Elliott, John H. *What is Social-Scientific Criticism?* Guides to Biblical Scholarship. Minneapolis: Fortress, 1993. A very helpful introduction to the application of the social sciences to NT study, with bibliography.

Fee, Gordon D. *New Testament Exegesis: A Handbook for Students and Pastors.* Rev. ed. Louisville: Westminster John Knox, 1993. A standard and very helpful, detailed guide to exegesis. This book is most useful for those working with the Greek text.

Green, Joel B., ed. *Hearing the New Testament: Strategies for Interpretation.* Grand Rapids: Eerdmans, 1995. A first-rate collection of essays on critical methods and issues of interpretation, for intermediate-level students. An excellent next-read for students of the NT.

Kennedy, George A. *New Testament Interpretation through Rhetorical Criticism.* Chapel Hill, N.C.: University of North Carolina Press, 1984. A standard guide to the use of classical rhetoric to interpret the NT, with applications to specific documents and shorter texts.

Mack, Burton L. *Rhetoric and the New Testament.* Guides to Biblical Scholarship. Minneapolis: Fortress, 1989. A guide to rhetorical criticism that draws on both classical approaches and modern theories, with illustrations of their use on specific texts.

McKnight, Scot, ed. *Introducing New Testament Interpretation.* Guides to New Testament Exegesis. Grand Rapids: Baker, 1989. A collection of brief essays on methods and issues, from an evangelical perspective, for beginning students.

Porter, Stanley E., ed. *Handbook to Exegesis of the New Testament.* Leiden: Brill, 1997. Essays on nearly all the exegetical approaches and methods and on their application to the various parts of the NT.

Schneiders, Sandra M. *The Revelatory Text: Interpreting the New Testament As Sacred Scripture.* 2d ed. Collegeville, Minn.: Liturgical, 1999. A sophisticated defense of the NT as fully human word and as locus of encounter with God, with theoretical consideration of an integrated model of interpretation that looks at the worlds behind, of, and before the text.

Stenger, Werner. *Introduction to New Testament Exegesis.* Ed. John W. Simpson Jr. Translated by Douglas W. Stott. Grand Rapids: Eerdmans, 1993. This translation and adaptation of a standard, hands-on text by a respected Roman Catholic NT scholar devotes a short chapter to each of several broad aspects of the historical-critical method (including textual criticism; structural analysis as a synchronic approach to the text; and the diachronic methods of tradition, source, redaction, and genre criticism). Then follow ten chapters illustrating these methods in practice (eight on gospel texts, one on two hymn texts, and one on the letter to Philemon). A helpful annotated bibliography is also included. A good next-read for students of the NT.

Weren, Wim. ***Windows on Jesus: Methods in Gospel Exegesis.*** Translated by John Bowden. Harrisburg, Pa.: Trinity, 1999. An excellent, comprehensive, and very accessible handbook to the varieties of contemporary approaches to the gospels, perfect for beginning and intermediate students of the gospels. Knowledge of Greek is not presumed.

Section 2. Resources for Understanding the Text

This section lists resources on the subjects of translations and textual criticism. It also lists editions of the Bible in Hebrew and Greek, multitranslation editions of the Bible, editions of the Bible in parallel format, and electronic versions of the Bible, many of which also contain resources for biblical study. For the issue of defining the limits of a text, consult the texts on exegetical method listed in section 1.

TRANSLATIONS

For discussion and analysis of various translations, see the following books:

Kubo, Sakae, and W. F. Specht. ***So Many Versions? Twentieth Century English Versions of the Bible.*** 2d ed. Grand Rapids: Zondervan, 1983. An overview and evaluation of major English-language translations, with a helpful appendix listing many others.

Lewis, Jack P. ***The English Bible from KJV to NIV.*** Grand Rapids: Baker, 1981; 2d ed., 1991. A comprehensive, detailed volume devoted to the (generally generous) evaluation of about twenty English translations; the 1991 edition includes chapters on the NKJV, REB, and NRSV.

Sheeley, Steven M., and Robert N. Nash Jr. ***The Bible in English Translation: An Essential Guide.*** Abingdon: Nashville,

1997. A basic but helpful guide to Bible translation and translations, plus the origins of the Bible and the development of the canon.

TEXTUAL CRITICISM

For discussion of the original text of the Bible, the practice of textual criticism, and the use of modern critical editions of the Hebrew and Greek texts, see:

Aland, Kurt, and Barbara Aland. *The Text of the New Testament.* Rev. and enlarged ed. Grand Rapids: Eerdmans, 1989. A helpful introduction to textual criticism and to the use of the critical apparatus of textual variants in the Nestle-Aland text of the NT.

Greenlee, J. Harold. *An Introduction to New Testament Textual Criticism.* Rev. ed. Peabody, Mass.: Hendrickson, 1995. A basic text.

McCarter, P. Kyle. *Textual Criticism: Recovering the Text of the Hebrew Bible.* Philadelphia: Fortress, 1986. A slim but authoritative volume.

Metzger, Bruce M. *The Text of the New Testament: Its Transmission, Corruption, and Restoration.* 3d enlarged ed. New York: Oxford University Press, 1992. A superb introduction to the art and science of textual criticism and to some of the principal NT manuscripts and early versions.

————, ed. *A Textual Commentary on the Greek New Testament.* 2d ed. New York: United Bible Societies, 1994. Presents the reasons for the decisions regarding the major text-critical issues of the standard critical text of the NT.

Weingreen, J. *Introduction to the Critical Study of the Bible.* Oxford: Oxford University Press, 1982. A basic introduction to textual criticism for students of the Hebrew Bible.

Würthwein, Emil. *The Text of the Old Testament: An Introduction to the Biblia Hebraica.* 2d ed. Grand Rapids: Eerdmans, 1995. A guide to texts, versions, and the use of the critical edition of the Hebrew Bible.

THE BIBLE IN HEBREW AND GREEK

Aland, B., K. Aland, J. Karavidopulos, C. M. Martini, and B. M. Metzger, eds. *The Greek New Testament.* 4th ed. Stuttgart: Deutsche Bibelgesellschaft, 1993. The standard text of the Greek NT, with a critical apparatus of significant textual variants that affect translation, distributed by the United Bible Societies. Abbreviated UBS[4].

Elliger, K. and W. Rudolph, eds. *Biblia Hebraica Stuttgartensia.* Stuttgart: Deutsche Bibelstiftung, 1968–1977; 1984. The standard text of the Hebrew Bible. Abbreviated *BHS.*

Jewish Publication Society. *JPS Hebrew-English Tanakh.* Philadelphia: Jewish Publication Society, 1999. Hebrew and English translation in parallel columns. (The preeminent Jewish translation into English.)

Nestle, E., and K. Aland, eds. *Novum Testamentum Graece.* 27th ed. Stuttgart: Deutsche Bibelgesellschaft, 1993. The standard text of the Greek NT with the most thorough critical apparatus of textual variants. The text itself is the same as the United Bible Societies' 3d and 4th editions. Available also in an edition with Greek and English on facing pages.

BIBLE PARALLELS

Aland, Kurt, ed. *Synopsis of the Four Gospels: Greek-English Edition of the Synopsis Quattuor Evangeliorum.* 6th ed. Stuttgart: United Bible Societies, 1983. This Greek-English synopsis of the Gospels in parallel columns is available also in English-only and in Greek *(Synopsis Quattuor Evangeliorum)* editions.

Francis, Fred O., and J. Paul Sampley. *Pauline Parallels.* 2d ed. Philadelphia: Fortress, 1984. A large spiral-bound book that sets out similar passages from the Pauline letters in parallel columns.

Throckmorton, Burton H., Jr., ed. *Gospel Parallels: A Comparison of the Synoptic Gospels.* 5th ed. Nashville: Nelson, 1992. The NRSV text of Matthew, Mark, and Luke in parallel columns.

ADDITIONAL TEXTS OF THE BIBLE

The Complete Parallel Bible: Containing the Old and New Testaments with the Apocrypha/Deuterocanonical Books. New York: Oxford University Press, 1993. Sets out the NRSV, REB, NAB, and NJB in parallel columns.

Kohlenberger, John R., III, ed. *The Contemporary Parallel New Testament.* New York: Oxford University Press, 1998. Sets out the NT text of eight translations in parallel columns: CEV, KJV, *The Message*, NASB, NCV (New Contemporary Version), NIV, NKJV, and NLT.

BIBLES ON CD-ROM

What follows is only a sample of Bibles available on CD-ROM and a brief introduction to some of those that make various tools available. More and better products will no doubt be produced in the coming years, and many of the products already on the market are constantly revised and expanded. Some products come as complete systems, while others come in a modular design whereby certain components or bundles of components may be purchased according to the needs of the user. It is wise to consult the manufacturer, and some end-users of various products, before making a purchase.

I have divided these Bible packages into two groups, those intended for sophisticated analysis of the texts in their original languages (which also make many translations available), and those intended for more general usage.

Sophisticated Original-Language Products

While almost every electronic Bible is capable of rapidly performing simple word searches, and many employ multiple versions augmented by secondary resources of varying quantity and quality, only a handful are capable of applying these resources to the original Greek and Hebrew texts. As the first choice for scholars who are able to read ancient languages (and students who hope to someday acquire such skills), these sophisticated products allow users to search and analyze both lexical (word) and syntactical (words-in-relationship) forms. Although a relatively recent innovation in biblical studies (Gramcord, the granddaddy of the three products reviewed here, dates from the mid-seventies), computerized analysis is increasingly being employed for exegesis, performing complex searches and analyses in mere seconds that used to require many hours of tedious research. The following three products are all capable of sophisticated original-language work.

> *Bible Works*. Hermeneutika. An incredibly comprehensive package, with various Greek and Hebrew texts, electronic analytical tools, lexicons, and many other first-rate resources. Comes with more than sixty translations in some twenty-two languages, including ASV, KJV, NAB, NAS95, NIV, NJB, NKJV, NLT, and NRSV. Sold as a complete package with all titles unlocked and can be installed directly on a hard drive.

> *Gramcord*. The Gramcord Institute. Designed especially for scholars and advanced students, these resources, which may be purchased in cost-effective, prepackaged bundles, include editions of the Greek and Hebrew texts, language tools, many translations (NASB, NAS95, NIV, NKJV, NRSV, RSV, etc.), and reference works. Resources are available in Windows and Apple Macintosh formats. Gramcord's modular format enables the initial purchase of either the Greek or Hebrew modules with the opportunity to add additional texts and resources at a later time.

> *Logos*. Logos Research Systems. The most extensive of all Bible-related and theological CD collections, the Logos system envisions a full electronic library. Logos makes available numerous translations and resources on several unlockable CD-ROMs, packaged in various bundles. Additional titles can then be purchased and unlocked. More than thirty translations (CEV, GNB, KJV, LB, *The Message*, NAB, NASB, NAS95, NIV, NJB, NKJV, NRSV, RSV, etc.) and hundreds of resources—including some of the very best in print, such

as *The Anchor Bible Dictionary*—are available in all price ranges.

Note: depending on the product bundle purchased, the prices for Gramcord and Logos vary from moderate to very high.

Products for More General Usage

macBible. Zondervan. This product makes several English translations (including KJV, NASB, NIV, and NRSV), as well as Greek and Hebrew texts, available to users of Apple Macintosh computers.

The NIV All-In-One Library. Zondervan. This package provides the KJV, NIV, NASB, and NRSV, plus *The NIV Study Bible* notes, the *NIV Exhaustive Concordance,* an interlinear NT, and other resources.

The Online Bible Deluxe. Online USA. This very large customizable package includes twelve English translations (including ASV, KJV, and RSV) and forty in other languages; *Biblia Hebraica* and three Greek texts; the Brown-Driver-Briggs lexicon; and several other reference works of variable quality.

PC Study Bible Complete Reference Library, Reference Library Plus, New Reference Library, and **Bible Reference Library.** Biblesoft. These packages include such translations as the ASV, KJV, LB, NASB, NIV, NKJV, and RSV, each with concordance, plus reference works. Some packages include language helps of variable quality. The "complete" version includes the standard Hebrew and Greek versions.

QuickVerse Deluxe, Deluxe Bible Reference Collection, and **New Bible Reference Collection.** Parsons. These packages contain numerous translations (usually including ASV, KJV, NIV, NKJV, NLT, NASB, and NRSV) plus a lot of generally out-of-date or low-quality reference tools. Most packages do, however, contain Strong's concordance.

Section 3. Resources for Surveying the Text

Several kinds of resources are especially helpful for expanding and refining one's initial survey of the text. These are handy reference works that provide a lot of good basic information and study aids in an economy of space and for use within an economy of time. They are particularly helpful for getting the "lay of the land" of a particular book and, later in the exegetical process, for identifying key aspects of the text. Introductions to the Old and New Testaments and one-volume Bible commentaries are included in this section. (Also useful for a brief overview are Bible dictionaries, which are listed in the next section on "Resources for Contextual Analysis.")

Not listed here are any "Bible handbooks." Although some of these works have merit, they generally attempt to be all things to all people, combining historical background information on "biblical times" with introductions to and summaries of biblical books, brief commentary on the text, and graphics. Unfortunately, most Bible handbooks are either not designed for serious students, are of poor quality, or both.

INTRODUCTIONS TO THE OLD AND NEW TESTAMENTS

Many introductions to one or the other of the two Testaments are in print. Below are several that are particularly popular and helpful. Each has useful bibliographies, too.

Old Testament/Hebrew Bible

Anderson, Bernhard W., and Katheryn Pfisterer Darr. ***Understanding the Old Testament.*** 4th ed., abridged and updated. Englewood Cliffs, N.J.: Prentice Hall, 1997. Still at more than six hundred pages, a new version of a balanced, classic introduction.

Bandstra, Barry. ***Reading the Old Testament: An Introduction to the Old Testament.*** Belmont, Calif.: Wadsworth, 1995. An introductory-level interpretation of the OT writings as historical, literary, and religious documents. Contains an excellent bibliography.

Birch, Bruce C., Walter Brueggemann, Terence E. Fretheim, and David L. Petersen. ***A Theological Introduction to the***

Old Testament. Nashville: Abingdon, 1999. A historical, canonical, and theological approach to the Christian OT.

Flanders, Henry J., Robert W. Crapps, and David A. Smith. ***People of the Covenant: An Introduction to the Hebrew Bible.*** 4th ed. New York: Oxford University Press, 1996. A basic introduction that follows a historical framework but places emphasis on the covenant people's theological interpretations of events and experiences.

Gottwald, Norman K. ***The Hebrew Bible: A Socio-Literary Introduction.*** Philadelphia: Fortress, 1985. An early and now classic approach emphasizing literary features and the political and social functions of the texts.

Hill, Andrew E., and J. H. Walton. ***A Survey of the Old Testament.*** 2d ed. Grand Rapids: Zondervan, 2000. A basic introduction from an evangelical perspective.

Laffey, Alice L. ***An Introduction to the Old Testament: A Feminist Perspective.*** Philadelphia: Fortress, 1988. A brief introduction to the main divisions of the Hebrew Bible with discussion of themes and texts within each from a feminist perspective.

LaSor, William Sanford, David Allan Hubbard, and Frederic Wm. Bush. With contributions by Leslie C. Allen et al. ***Old Testament Survey: The Message, Form, and Background of the Old Testament.*** 2d ed. Grand Rapids: Eerdmans, 1996. An excellent basic introduction written from a critical evangelical perspective, with emphasis on literary structure and theological message.

McKenzie, Steven L., and M. Patrick Graham, eds. ***The Hebrew Bible Today: An Introduction to Critical Issues.*** Louisville: Westminster John Knox, 1998. A survey of the books of the OT or Hebrew Bible with respect to issues such as authorship, structure, sources, and themes.

New Testament

Barr, David L. ***New Testament Story: An Introduction.*** 2d ed. Belmont, Calif.: Wadsworth, 1995. An introduction that takes social-scientific and rhetorical approaches seriously while looking at the three "worlds of the text" (behind, within, and in front of).

Brown, Raymond E. *An Introduction to the New Testament.* New York: Doubleday, 1997. A masterful, library-like introduction and mini-commentary, largely in the historical-critical tradition but with appreciation for narrative and other approaches.

Ehrman, Bart D. *The New Testament: A Historical Introduction to the Early Christian Writings.* 2d ed. New York: Oxford University Press, 2000. A user-friendly, well-written survey that is "historically rather than confessionally oriented," with excellent charts, illustrations, and brief annotated bibliographies.

Gundry, Robert. *A Survey of the New Testament.* 3d ed. Grand Rapids: Zondervan, 1994. A basic, standard introduction from an evangelical perspective.

Johnson, Luke Timothy, with Todd Penner. *The New Testament Writings: An Interpretation.* Rev. ed. Philadelphia: Fortress, 1999. A standard, elegantly written introduction with emphasis on the social world and theological message of the text and on early Christian experience.

McDonald, Lee Martin, and Stanley Porter. *Early Christianity and Its Sacred Literature.* Peabody, Mass.: Hendrickson, 2000. A comprehensive and well-illustrated introduction to early Christian literature in context, including color photos as well as charts and maps.

Pregeant, Russell. *Engaging the New Testament: An Interdisciplinary Introduction.* Minneapolis: Augsburg Fortress, 1995. A creative introduction that incorporates a wide variety of approaches to reading the NT.

The Entire Bible

Most books that cover the entire Bible do so very superficially; one major exception is the following:

Alter, Robert, and Frank Kermode, eds. *The Literary Guide to the Bible.* Cambridge, Mass.: Harvard University Press,

1987. A collection of superb essays on the literary genre and features of the various biblical books.

ONE-VOLUME BIBLE COMMENTARIES

A one-volume Bible commentary is a commentary on the entire Bible in one volume (as opposed to a commentary in one volume on one particular book). This kind of reference book is helpful for getting acquainted with a biblical book and passage but is generally not sufficiently in-depth or extensive to be useful for serious research. This is not to say, however, that such a book is unscholarly; indeed, the best ones are written by the best biblical scholars. These scholars cannot, however, fully develop or argue their perspective in such limited space.

Far and away the most comprehensive of the one-volume commentaries is the revised edition of *The New Jerome Biblical Commentary* (Englewood Cliffs, N.J.: Prentice Hall, 1990), edited by the great Roman Catholic scholars Raymond E. Brown, Joseph A. Fitzmyer, and Roland E. Murphy. This volume is a library within a book. At nearly 1500 pages of fine print, it includes scholarly commentary on the entire Bible, including, of course, the deuterocanonical books; introductions (sometimes brief, but sometimes quite lengthy) to and detailed outlines of each book; and, as a bonus, more than twenty-five additional, in-depth articles on important topics in biblical studies. These topics include introductions to the various kinds of biblical literature, hermeneutics, biblical geography and archaeology, modern criticism (study) of the Bible, and aspects of the thought (theology) of each Testament and of some of its key writers (e.g., Paul and John). The articles include excellent, extensive bibliographies, as do each of the commentaries proper. Though Roman Catholic in authorship, it is ecumenical in tone. Its only drawback is that the prose is sometimes very technical and dense, making for challenging reading.

Another helpful one-volume commentary is *Harper's Bible Commentary* (rev. ed.; San Francisco: Harper & Row, 2000), edited by James L. Mays and written by members of the Society of Biblical Literature (as in the case of *The HarperCollins Study Bible*). Though less thorough than the *New Jerome*, it is also more user-friendly. In addition to introductions to and commentary on each of the biblical books, including the Apocrypha, this resource has several general articles, introductory articles on the main divisions of the Bible, and several dozen short essays within various commentary articles. It also contains a system of cross-references to *Harper's Bible Dictionary.*

A standard for a half-century has been the **New Bible Commentary,** now in the *21st Century Edition* (= 4th ed.; Downers Grove, Ill.: InterVarsity, 1994), edited by Donald A. Carson et al. Evangelical in orientation, the new edition is based on the NIV text. All articles from the last edition (1970) have been revised or replaced. The historically conservative approach of many of the writers for previous editions is still present in some articles but is offered more cautiously and less centrally; the text itself is center stage. A reliable and solid piece of work, this is a good place to begin one's introduction to the biblical texts. The format, however, is less contemporary and visually appealing than some other works.

A feminist perspective is provided by the **Women's Bible Commentary** (Louisville: Westminster John Knox, 1992; expanded edition, with Apocrypha, 1998), edited by Carol A. Newsom and Sharon H. Ringe. This is not a full one-volume commentary but one that comments only on the passages of a book that the commentator judges to be "of particular relevance to women"—especially texts that speak about women or have female characters. Some short articles and brief bibliographies for each book are included. Sometimes offering an unconventional perspective within a hermeneutic of suspicion, these brief articles can be used with other perspectives within the exegetical process.

BIBLE DICTIONARIES

As noted above, also helpful for the purposes of surveying a passage within its document are the entries on biblical books in Bible dictionaries, which are discussed below under the resources for contextual analysis.

Section 4. Resources for Contextual Analysis

The following resources—Bible dictionaries, studies of the "biblical world," and atlases—assist the exegete especially in analyzing the historical, social, and cultural contexts of the Bible. The articles on particular biblical books (e.g., Exodus) in Bible dictionaries can also be brief but helpful guides to the general literary and rhetorical context of a passage. For more in-depth analysis of literary context, the reader should consult the one-volume commentaries listed in the previous section and especially the full-length commentaries described in the next section.

BIBLE DICTIONARIES

A Bible dictionary is an alphabetically arranged encyclopedia of biblical names, places, events, customs, ideas, books, and other topics, as well as (sometimes) technical terms related to the study of the Bible. Bible dictionaries have several uses, such as providing an overview of the historical situation and identifying key figures, events, and customs that appear in a passage. They can serve also as handy sources for surveying the book within which a passage is found.

There are both one-volume and multivolume dictionaries. Of special usefulness and quality are the following:

> Achtemeier, Paul, gen. ed. *HarperCollins Bible Dictionary.* Rev. ed. San Francisco: HarperSanFrancisco, 1996. Contains brief, lucid, up-to-date entries as well as numerous extended essays on selected topics. The entries for biblical books contain detailed outlines.

> Bromiley, Geoffrey W., ed. *The International Standard Bible Encyclopedia.* 4 vols. Rev. ed. Grand Rapids: Eerdmans, 1979–1988. The revision of a 1929 conservative classic. Lavishly illustrated with more than three hundred maps, hundreds of illustrations and photos, and several sections of full-color plates. Evangelical in orientation, it contains good bibliographies on many of its topics. Abbreviated *ISBE.*

Douglas, J. D., and N. Hillyer, eds. ***The Illustrated Bible Dictionary.*** 3 vols. Downers Grove, Ill.: InterVarsity, 1980. Based on the second edition of the *New Bible Dictionary* (see below), this lavishly illustrated mini-encyclopedia welcomes the reader into the world of the text with hundreds of superb, colorful photographs, illustrations, and maps to accompany its entries.

Freedman, David Noel, gen. ed. ***The Anchor Bible Dictionary.*** New York: Doubleday, 1992. 6 vols. This encyclopedia of more than six thousand entries, some the equivalent of small books, is an authoritative guide to scholarly knowledge of and perspectives on every Bible-related topic. Its discussions of specific biblical books are particularly helpful at the survey and contextual analysis stages of exegesis. Available also on CD-ROM. Abbreviated *ABD*.

————, ed. ***Eerdmans Dictionary of the Bible.*** Grand Rapids: Eerdmans, 2000. This first-rate dictionary has almost five thousand contributions from more than six hundred scholars representing diverse scholarly and theological approaches. It is billed as a "rapid-response reference work."

Marshall, I. Howard et al., eds. ***New Bible Dictionary.*** 3d ed. Downers Grove, Ill.: InterVarsity, 1996. A very thorough and competent volume in the critical evangelical tradition.

Mills, Watson, gen. ed. ***Mercer Dictionary of the Bible.*** Macon, Ga.: Mercer University Press, 1990. Produced under the guidance of Baptist biblical scholars, but ecumenical in tone and substance.

Of special interest to students of the NT is the following series from a critical, ecumenical, evangelical perspective. All of these dictionaries are available, bundled with other InterVarsity reference works, on one CD-ROM.

Evans, Craig A., and Stanley E. Porter, eds. ***Dictionary of New Testament Background.*** Downers Grove, Ill.: InterVarsity, 2000.

Green, Joel B., Scot McKnight, and I. Howard Marshall, eds. ***Dictionary of Jesus and the Gospels.*** Downers Grove, Ill.: InterVarsity, 1992.

Hawthorne, Gerald F., Ralph P. Martin, and Daniel G. Reid, eds. *Dictionary of Paul and His Letters.* Downers Grove, Ill.: InterVarsity, 1993.

Martin, Ralph P., and Peter H. Davids, eds. *Dictionary of the Later New Testament and its Developments.* Downers Grove, Ill.: InterVarsity, 1997.

General Books on the "Biblical Worlds"

Coogan, Michael D., ed. *The Oxford History of the Biblical World.* New York: Oxford University Press, 1998. Twelve scholars contribute to this elegant volume on the social, economic, political, literary, architectural, and ideological worlds of the Bible. Includes more than two hundred photos (twenty-five in color) as well as drawings and maps, plus annotated bibliographies.

Neusner, Jacob, and William Scott Green, eds. *Dictionary of Judaism in the Biblical Period.* Peabody, Mass.: Hendrickson, 1999. Defines terms, ideas, people, places, and practices of the Jewish people from the time of the formation of the Pentateuch to the Babylonian Talmud.

Books on the Old Testament Historical and Social Contexts

Albertz, Rainer. *A History of Israelite Religion in the Old Testament Period.* Translated by John Bowden. 2 vols. The Old Testament Library. Louisville: Westminster John Knox, 1994. A thorough social history of Israel, period-by-period, in interaction with surrounding cultures and with special emphasis on politics, worship, family life, piety, and community identity.

Clements, Roland E., ed. *The World of Ancient Israel: Sociological, Anthropological, and Political Perspectives.* Cambridge: Cambridge University Press, 1989. A helpful collection of essays on the impact of these perspectives on the understanding of the Bible and the history of its peoples.

Soden, Wolfram von. *The Ancient Orient: An Introduction to the Study of the Ancient Near East.* Grand Rapids: Eerdmans, 1994. A helpful survey of the world within which the OT texts were created.

Woude, A. S. van der. *The World of the Old Testament.* Bible Handbook, Vol 2. Grand Rapids: Eerdmans, 1989. A superb collection of articles in encyclopedia-type format, with excellent bibliographies.

BOOKS ON THE NEW TESTAMENT HISTORICAL AND SOCIAL CONTEXTS

Boring, M. Eugene, Klaus Berger, and Carsten Colpe, eds. *Hellenistic Commentary to the New Testament.* Nashville: Abingdon, 1995. A collection of texts from the Hellenistic world that parallel or illustrate the NT, arranged in order from Matthew to Revelation. Includes cross-references and indexes.

Cohen, Shaye. *From the Maccabees to the Mishnah.* Philadelphia: Westminster, 1987. A clear, concise, and authoritative overview of early Judaism.

Ferguson, Everett. *Backgrounds of Early Christianity.* Rev. ed. Grand Rapids: Eerdmans, 1993. An excellent treatment of politics, religion, and philosophy in the Hellenistic-Roman context.

Jeffers, James S. *The Greco-Roman World of the New Testament Era: Exploring the Background of Early Christianity.* Downer's Grove, Ill.: InterVarsity, 1999. A superb survey of all aspects of life and society in the Greco-Roman era.

Koester, Helmut. *Introduction to the New Testament.* **Vol. 1.** *History, Culture, and Religion of the Hellenistic Age.* Rev. ed. Philadelphia: Fortress, 1995. A thorough, standard study of the world in which the NT was born, with emphasis on the non-Jewish dimensions.

Malina, Bruce J. *The New Testament World: Insights from Cultural Anthropology.* Rev. ed. Louisville: Westminster John Knox, 1993. Uses anthropological models to interpret the pivotal values of honor and shame, personality, social status, kinship and marriage, and purity in the first century and in NT texts.

Osiek, Carolyn. *What Are They Saying about the Social Setting of the New Testament?* Rev. and expanded ed. New York: Paulist, 1992. A survey of trends in various areas of NT research.

Stambaugh, John E., and David L. Balch. *The New Testament in Its Social Environment.* Library of Early Christianity. Philadelphia: Westminster, 1986. A survey of mobility, economy, society, and urban life.

ATLASES

In addition to the printed volumes listed here, many electronic and online atlases now exist. Especially helpful, for example, is the atlas available in the Logos packages, which in some versions is hyperlinked to the biblical text.

The Macmillan Bible Atlas. New York: Macmillan, 1993.

May, Herbert G. *Oxford Bible Atlas.* 3d ed. New York: Oxford University Press, 1984.

Pritchard, James B., ed. *The Harper Concise Atlas of the Bible.* San Francisco: HarperCollins, 1991.

Section 5. Resources for Formal Analysis

The following resources are useful handbooks for understanding the forms, genres, structures, and other literary aspects of texts that you identify in the process of exegesis. The general insights of these books may be applied to your specific text. In addition to the books listed below, see Alter and Kermode, *The Literary Guide to the Bible* (section 3 above) for literary genres, and most recent commentaries for discussion of literary and rhetorical structure.

Alter, Robert. *The Art of Biblical Narrative.* New York: Basic Books, 1981. A classic treatment.

————. *The Art of Biblical Poetry.* New York: Basic Books, 1985. Another classic treatment of its subject.

Aune, David. *The New Testament in Its Literary Environment.* Library of Early Christianity. Philadelphia: Westminster, 1987. A superb analysis of the literary genres of the NT writings in context.

Bailey, James L., and Lyle D. Vander Broek. *Literary Forms in the New Testament: A Handbook.* Louisville: Westminster John Knox, 1992. A helpful guide to the specific forms found in the various kinds of NT documents.

Berlin, Adele. *The Dynamics of Biblical Parallelism.* Bloomington, Ind.: Indiana University Press, 1985. An important work on OT parallelism that uses insights from modern linguistics.

Dorsey, David A. *The Literary Structure of the Old Testament: A Commentary on Genesis to Malachi.* Grand Rapids: Baker, 1999. A novel "commentary" that considers the literary structure of each book and how that structure affects interpretation of particular texts.

Fee, Gordon D., and Douglas Stuart. *How to Read the Bible for All Its Worth: A Guide to Understanding the Bible.* 2d ed. Grand Rapids: Zondervan. 1993. A helpful, basic introduction to the rules of exegesis and interpretation for the various literary genres (epistles, gospels, parables, law, psalms, etc.) of the Bible, written from an evangelical perspective.

Lohfink, Gerhard. *The Bible: Now I Get It! A Form-Criticism Handbook.* Translated by Daniel Coogan. Garden City, N.Y.: Doubleday, 1979. A delightful introduction to various literary forms in the Bible, presented in connection with different forms of communication in daily life.

McKnight, Edgar V. *What Is Form Criticism?* Philadelphia: Fortress, 1969. A brief, standard introduction to the origins, practice, and critique of form criticism of the gospels.

Ryken, Leland. *Words of Delight: A Literary Introduction to the Bible.* 2d ed. Grand Rapids: Baker, 1992. A very insightful discussion of biblical narrative, poetry, and smaller literary forms, including encomium, proverb, satire, drama, and the many literary forms found in the gospels (parables, call stories, miracle stories, etc.).

Tucker, Gene M. *Form Criticism of the Old Testament.* Guides to Biblical Scholarship. Philadelphia: Fortress, 1971. A basic guide to the origins and application of form criticism to the OT.

In addition to the works cited above, students of the OT/ Hebrew Bible will be interested in a series published by Eerdmans, entitled The Forms of the Old Testament Literature, edited by Rolf Knierim and Gene M. Tucker.

Section 6. Resources for Detailed Analysis

There are numerous tools available for detailed analysis of the text. In this section we describe handbooks on detailed analysis, concordances, grammars, dictionaries and similar resources, journals, and commentaries. Those who wish to find such resources on CD-ROM should look at the information on "Bibles on CD-ROM" under section 2, "Resources for Understanding the Text," above.

HANDBOOKS AND OTHER WORKS ON DETAILED TEXTUAL ANALYSIS

In addition to chapters in books on exegetical method (see section 1 on "Resources for Understanding the Task") on such topics as lexical analysis, grammar and syntax, and redaction criticism, as well as books on the analysis of specific genres (see section 5 on "Resources for Formal Analysis"), the following books may be of value in expanding one's tools for doing detailed analysis.

Barr, James. *The Semantics of Biblical Language.* Oxford: Oxford University Press, 1961. The classic treatment of the abuse and proper use of words, grammar, and other linguistic phenomena in biblical exegesis and theology more generally.

Bock, Darrell L. **"New Testament Word Analysis."** Pages 97–113 in *Introducing New Testament Interpretation.* Ed. Scot McKnight. Guides to New Testament Exegesis. Grand Rapids: Baker, 1989. A concise, insightful guide to the practices and pitfalls of word analysis, appropriate for beginning students, especially those using the original languages.

Cotterell, Peter, and Max Turner. *Linguistics and Biblical Interpretation.* Downers Grove, Ill.: InterVarsity, 1989. A superb guide to applying the principles of modern linguistics to the study of the Bible, including words, grammar, sentences, discourses, and nonliteral language. Appropriate for intermediate and advanced readers.

Fewell, Danna N., ed. *Reading between Texts: Intertextuality and the Hebrew Bible.* Louisville: Westminster John Knox, 1992. A collection of articles on the phenomenon of textual borrowing within the Hebrew Bible.

Horrell, David, ed. *Social-Scientific Approaches to New Testament Interpretation.* Edinburgh: T&T Clark, 1999. A collection of classic essays in the field, with bibliographies and an introduction to the social-scientific approach.

Kingsbury, Jack Dean, ed. *Gospel Interpretation: Narrative-Critical and Social-Scientific Approaches.* Harrisburg, Pa.: Trinity, 1997. A collection of articles on each of the four gospels that reveals the methods and insights of recent synchronic approaches to detailed analysis of the gospels. The articles do not focus on the exegesis of short texts but rather on a specific gospel as a whole. Nonetheless, the presentation of the methods in action is extremely useful for beginning to advanced students.

Patte, Daniel. *What Is Structural Exegesis?* Philadelphia: Fortress, 1976. An introduction to the theory and practice of structural exegesis applied to the NT.

Perrin, Norman. *What Is Redaction Criticism?* Guides to Biblical Scholarship. Philadelphia: Fortress, 1969. A classic, brief exposition of the origins, practice, and significance of the method, with samples of its use on the gospels.

Silva, Moisés. *Biblical Words and Their Meaning: An Introduction to Lexical Semantics.* Rev. ed. Grand Rapids: Zondervan, 1994. A basic but very helpful introduction to the study of words, informed by modern principles of linguistics.

CONCORDANCES

A concordance is an alphabetical listing of the words that occur in a body of literature, with a reference (e.g., 2 Kings 3:4) and usually a brief context line. A "complete" concordance lists every word, but not every occurrence; an "exhaustive" concordance lists every occurrence of every word (though not with context lines for frequent words like "and"); and an "analytical" concordance of an English translation somehow indicates the occurrences of words according to their equivalents in the original language (e.g., under "love," several kinds of entries appear, corresponding to the various Hebrew and Greek words that are translated "love"). Some concordances provide numbering systems connecting words in the English translation with the words in the original language. Many kinds of concordances are now available electronically, both on CD and online.

Concordances of the Bible in the Original Languages

Bachmann, H., and W. Slaby. *Computer Concordance to the Novum Testamentum Graece of Nestle-Aland, 26th edition, and to the Greek New Testament, 3rd edition.* 2d ed. Berlin: de Gruyter, 1985. The standard Greek NT concordance, computer-generated and printed on large pages with very clear type and formatting.

Clapp, Philip S., Barbara Friberg, and Timothy Friberg, eds. *Analytical Concordance of the Greek New Testament.* 2 vols. Grand Rapids: Baker, 1991. A concordance to the actual forms and structures of the Greek words in the NT. For students interested in issues of grammar.

Even-Shoshan, Abraham, ed. *A New Concordance of the Bible.* 2d ed. Jerusalem: Kiryat Sefer, 1983; Grand Rapids: Baker, 1989. A standard concordance to the Hebrew Bible.

Lisowsky, Gerhard. ***Konkordanz zum hebraeischen Alten Testament.*** Stuttgart: Württ. Bibelanstalt, 1958. A computer-generated concordance to the *Biblia Hebraica.* Introductory material in English is included.

Mandelkern, Solomon. ***Veteris Testamenti Concordantiae Hebraicae atque Chaldaicae.*** 8th ed. Jerusalem: Schocken, 1969. A standard concordance to the OT.

Moulton, W. F., A. S. Geden, and H. K. Moulton. ***A Concordance to the Greek Testament.*** 5th ed. Edinburgh: T&T Clark, 1978; repr. Grand Rapids: Baker, 1997. A standard concordance to the NT.

Concordances to Selected English Translations

Goodrick, Edward W., and John R. Kohlenberger III, eds. ***NIV Exhaustive Concordance.*** Grand Rapids: Zondervan, 1990. A computer-generated concordance with a numbering system to indicate the underlying word in the original language.

Hartdegen, Stephen J., gen. ed. ***Nelson's Complete Concordance of the New American Bible.*** Collegeville, Minn.: Liturgical, 1977. Does not include the NAB update to the NT.

Kohlenberger, John R., III, ed. ***The NRSV Concordance Unabridged, Including the Apocryphal/Deuterocanonical Books.*** Grand Rapids: Zondervan 1991. A computer-generated concordance with an additional "topical index," but no references to the original languages.

Strong, James. ***Strong's Exhaustive Concordance.*** Various publishers, dates, and formats. Contains a widely used numbering system keyed to the KJV.

Thomas, Robert L., ed. ***New American Standard Exhaustive Concordance of the Bible, Hebrew-Aramaic and Greek Dictionaries.*** Nashville: Holman, 1981. A concordance keyed to the original version of the NASB that includes the Strong numbering system.

Whitaker, Richard E., and James Goehring, eds. ***The Eerdmans Analytical Concordance to the Revised Standard Version of*** *the Bible.* Grand Rapids: Eerdmans, 1988. A computer-generated concordance in which every entry is accompanied by the original-language word it translates, which in turn is numbered. The numbers take the reader to an index of all the words from the original languages.

GRAMMARS

Blass, F., and A. Debrunner. *A Greek Grammar of the New Testament and Other Early Christian Literature.* Translated by and rev. R. W. Funk. Chicago: University of Chicago Press, 1961. The standard reference grammar for the NT writings. Abbreviated BDF.

Gesenius, W., and E. Kautzsch. *Gesenius' Hebrew Grammar.* 17th ed. Oxford: Oxford University Press, 1983. An older but standard work.

Joüon, Paul. *A Grammar of Biblical Hebrew.* Translated and rev. by T. Muraoka. 2 vols. Rome: Pontifical Biblical Institute, 1991. A comprehensive treatment first published in 1923.

Wallace, Daniel B. *Greek Grammar Beyond the Basics: An Exegetical Syntax of the New Testament.* Grand Rapids: Zondervan, 1996. A first-rate, user-friendly handbook to the details of Greek grammar and their importance for exegesis, with charts, indexes, and bibliographies.

Waltke, Bruce K., and M. O'Connor. *An Introduction to Biblical Hebrew Syntax.* Winona Lake, Ind.: Eisenbrauns, 1990. A massive intermediate grammar, with copious illustrations from the biblical text.

DICTIONARIES/LEXICONS, WORDBOOKS, AND ENCYCLOPEDIAS

Works That Can Be Used with Minimal or No Knowledge of the Original Language(s)

In addition to the works listed below, see especially *The Anchor Bible Dictionary* listed above in section 4, "Resources for Contextual Analysis."

Brown, Colin, ed. *The New International Dictionary of New Testament Theology.* 4 vols. Grand Rapids: Zondervan, 1975–1978. Articles on words of theological significance in the NT, arranged alphabetically by English word. Abbreviated *NIDNTT.* Also available on CD-ROM.

VanGemeren, Willem A., ed. *The New International Dictionary of Old Testament Theology and Exegesis.* 5 vols. Grand Rapids: Zondervan, 1997. Articles on words of theological significance in the OT, arranged alphabetically by English word. Abbreviated *NIDOTTE.* Also available on CD-ROM.

Works That Require Facility in the Original Language(s)

Old Testament

Botterweck, G. Johannes, Helmer Ringgren, and Hans-Josef Fabry, eds. *Theological Dictionary of the Old Testament.* 10+ vols. Translated by John T. Willis. Grand Rapids: Eerdmans, 1974–. A "word-study" approach to the key Hebrew and Aramaic terms in the Bible, this set (incomplete as of this writing), like the *TDNT* (see below), makes many contributions but also fosters some misunderstanding as a "wordbook." As an encyclopedia, however, it is a gold mine of information. Abbreviated *TDOT.*

Brown, F., S. R. Driver, and C. A. Briggs. *Hebrew and English Lexicon of the Old Testament.* Orig. 1906. Repr. Peabody, Mass.: Hendrickson, 1999. A classic Hebrew Bible lexicon. Abbreviated BDB.

Holladay, William L. *A Concise Hebrew and Aramaic Lexicon of the Old Testament.* Grand Rapids: Eerdmans, 1972. A handy basic lexicon for students.

Jenni, Ernst, and Claus Westermann, eds. *Theological Lexicon of the Old Testament.* 3 vols. Translated by M. Biddle. Peabody, Mass.: Hendrickson, 1997. An excellent resource for the theological vocabulary and concepts of the OT.

Koehler, Ludwig, Walter Baumgartner, and Johann Jakob Stamm. *The Hebrew and Aramaic Lexicon of the Old Testament.* Translated and ed. by M. E. J. Richardson et al. 4

vols. Leiden: Brill, 1994–2000. A thorough, scholarly, standard lexicon, also available on CD-ROM. Abbreviated *HALOT.*

New Testament

Bauer, Walter. *A Greek-English Lexicon of the New Testament and Other Early Christian Literature.* 3d ed. Edited and revised by F. W. Danker. Translated and adapted by W. F. Arndt, F. W. Gingrich, and F. W. Danker. Chicago: University of Chicago Press, 2000. This edition, abbreviated BDAG (Bauer-Danker-Arndt-Gingrich), is a completely revised version of the standard philologically oriented NT lexicon. The 1979 edition, abbreviated BAGD (Bauer-Arndt-Gingrich-Danker), is frequently cited.

Friberg, Timothy, Barbara Friberg, and Neva F. Miller. *Analytical Lexicon of the Greek New Testament.* Grand Rapids: Baker, 2000. An alphabetical presentation of every Greek form found in all the major editions of the Greek NT, providing definitions of all root words and "parsings" (analyses) of all forms.

Kittel, Gerhard, and Gerhard Friedrich, eds. *Theological Dictionary of the New Testament.* Translated and ed. by G. W. Bromiley. 10 vols. Grand Rapids: Eerdmans, 1964–1976. Available also on CD-ROM. An "encyclopaedia of New Testament theology organized alphabetically on the basis of its lexical stock" (Cotterell and Turner, *Linguistics and Biblical Interpretation,* 108). Must be used with some caution because it confuses the sense of words in context and theological concepts/history of ideas. Best used as a resource for the semantic range and usage of words in antiquity. Abbreviated *TDNT.*

Liddell, H. G., and R. Scott. *A Greek-English Lexicon.* Rev. ed. Aug. by H. S. Jones. 9th rev. ed. Oxford: Clarendon, 1996. The standard lexicon of classical Greek. Abbreviated LSJ.

Louw, Johannes P., and Eugene Nida, eds. *Greek-English Lexicon of the New Testament Based on Semantic Domains.* 2d ed. New York: United Bible Societies, 1989. A dictionary that focuses not on the history of words but on semantic relationships. A good complement to the traditional lexicon. Now available on CD-ROM from a company called iExalt.

Spicq, Ceslas. ***Theological Lexicon of the New Testament.*** Translated by James Ernest. 3 vols. Peabody, Mass.: Hendrickson, 1994. An excellent resource for the theological vocabulary and concepts of the NT.

JOURNALS

Following is a brief description of some leading journals in the field of biblical studies. They are useful for many topics, but most especially for detailed treatment of texts.

Biblica—technical articles published in several languages

Biblical Archaeology Review—readable articles on discoveries and scholarly issues (not intended primarily for scholars)

Biblical Theology Bulletin—despite the title, a journal devoted primarily to social-scientific perspectives

Catholic Biblical Quarterly—contributions from an ecumenical group of scholars, largely in the historical-critical tradition

Ex Auditu—exegetical and thematic articles with a strong theological interest

Expository Times—British publication, international in scope, with brief but helpful articles, reviews, and surveys of current trends in scholarship

Harvard Theological Review—articles in the historical-critical tradition

Horizons in Biblical Theology—articles on methods, issues, and themes in biblical theology

Interpretation—exegetical and thematic articles with a strong theological and homiletical interest

Journal for the Study of the New Testament—technical articles from a variety of perspectives and countries, emphasizing literary and theological concerns

Journal for the Study of the Old Testament—technical articles from a variety of perspectives and countries, emphasizing literary and theological concerns

Journal of Biblical Literature—technical articles largely in the historical-critical tradition

Journal of Theological Studies—frequent articles related to biblical studies

New Testament Studies—an international journal of technical articles representing various approaches to exegesis

Novum Testamentum—an international journal of technical articles representing various approaches to exegesis

Review and Expositor—exegetical and thematic articles

Scottish Journal of Theology—a theological journal with strong biblical and hermeneutical interests

Semeia—an "experimental" journal focusing on new and recent approaches and methods

Vetus Testamentum—an international journal of technical articles representing various approaches to exegesis

In the coming years, an increasing number of journals will no doubt be available online. The American Theological Library Association (ATLA) is in the process of digitizing fifty years worth of approximately fifty theological periodicals for access by the public. Among these are several devoted to biblical studies, including *Catholic Biblical Quarterly, Interpretation, Journal for the Study of the New Testament, Journal for the Study of the Old Testament, Journal of Biblical Literature, Novum Testamentum,* and *Vetus Testamentum.* Further information is available at the ATLA website: http://rosetta. atla-certr.org/CERTR/ATLAS/FAQ.html#journals

COMMENTARIES

Of the making of commentaries there truly is no end. Even the experts who write them complain that there are too many, but the production line is not slowing down. At a recent conference of biblical scholars, a friend asked, "Don't tell me you're writing a commentary on Philippians, too. Everyone I know is!" (Fortunately, I was not.) In this section we consider commentaries that are devoted (generally) to one book of the Bible (or perhaps two or three short books), as opposed to one-volume commentaries, which were discussed in section 3 on "survey."

Commentaries are of several types, having a wide variety of purposes and perspectives. Some are "devotional" or "spiritual" in nature, intended to nourish the religious life of their readers and often (though not always) prepared by authors with little or no scholarly expertise in their subject. Similar to these, but more often written by acknowledged experts, are "homiletical" commentaries, by which I mean either collections of sermons on biblical books or commentary intended primarily to provide responsible insights for preachers. These two kinds of commentaries have their place in the life of faith, in the theological reflection of faith communities, and in the task of exegesis broadly understood as an ongoing conversation that provokes reflection on the text. Indeed, some of the most important commentaries of all time are homiletical, such as the sermons of Augustine, Chrysostom, and Calvin. Unfortunately, most modern exegetes avoid such commentaries, but they do so only to their own detriment. The literary, historical, and especially theological insights of these authors are often profound and provocative.

The following series attempts to capture the exegetical insights of the church fathers on the Bible:

> Oden, Thomas C., gen. ed. ***Ancient Christian Commentary on Scripture.*** 27 vols. [scheduled]. Downers Grove, Ill.: InterVarsity, 1998–. A multivolume set of anthologies of quotations from early Christian writers on each book of the Bible.

The sermons and commentaries of some of the great theologians and biblical interpreters of the church include those of Augustine, Chrysostom, Martin Luther, John Calvin,

John Wesley, and Matthew Henry. These works can be found in various editions. Calvin's complete works, and an extensive collection of Luther's works, are now available on CD-ROM, as are those of the early church fathers.

For the purposes of careful, detailed analysis, contemporary exegetes generally turn to commentaries prepared by modern biblical scholars. These, too, fall into various categories. Although they are all prepared by scholars working with the Bible in its original languages, the commentaries themselves may be on either the Greek or Hebrew text, on a specific translation (such as the NRSV), or on the commentator's own translation (as in the case of *The Anchor Bible* series). Exegetes who do not read the original languages can usually still profit from a commentary on the Greek or Hebrew text, but they will often miss nuanced insights, may find the discussion or argument difficult to follow, and may become annoyed at the quantity of Greek or Hebrew in the commentary. For this reason, many commentators choose to base their analysis on a translation and refer to the original languages through the transliteration of terms. When transliteration is used in abundance, however, readers who do not know the original language can easily experience the same problems as they do with commentaries filled with Greek and Hebrew words.

Scholarly commentaries also vary as to their approach and purpose. Some, especially those from the first seventy-five years of the twentieth century, are primarily interested in diachronic exegesis, or the origin and development of the text. These commentaries emphasize source, form, tradition, and redaction criticism as well as historical and literary parallels to the text in the ancient world. Such commentaries are still being produced, using the results of current historical, philological, archaeological, and other scientific research to analyze the text. These commentaries may be referred to as "historical-critical" commentaries.

A recent offshoot of the traditional historically oriented commentary is the "social-science" or "social-scientific" commentary. This kind of commentary emphasizes the importance of understanding the social and cultural dimensions of the text and of the communities by which and in which it was produced. Most recent commentaries, however, even those that stress the social context of a writing, are likely to place greater or even exclusive emphasis on the final form of the text rather than on its origins and development. The writers of these commentaries are engaged primarily in synchronic exegesis. They emphasize literary and rhetorical criticism. Indeed, one of the most recent trends has been to combine social-scientific and rhetorical criticism to produce "socio-rhetorical" commentaries.

Still other commentaries, while benefitting from some or all of the possible approaches to exegesis, emphasize the substantive literary and theological content of the final form of the text. This eclectic approach is likely the one that most beginning exegetes will adopt in some form, simply because they cannot possibly master all the technical critical methods. Nevertheless, exegetes can and should benefit from a variety of kinds of commentaries, using the insights of several to correct, refine, and expand their own exegesis of the text.

Commentaries are published either (1) in series, in which generally one volume is dedicated to one biblical book; (2) in multivolume sets, in which several books are treated in each volume of a set; or (3) as "stand-alone" volumes, or works published independently of a series or set. Following are several of the current series available (many of which are incomplete) and a few of the multivolume sets. Space does not permit discussion of the many fine stand-alone commentaries.

Series

The ***Abingdon New Testament Commentaries*** series (Nashville: Abingdon, 1996–) represents superior scholarship in an accessible format. Each volume has an introduction, unit-by-unit commentary on the text, an annotated bibliography, and a subject index. Commentators are sensitive to literary, historical, and theological dimensions of the text.

The Anchor Bible (AB) series (Garden City, N.Y.: Doubleday, 1964–) is an interfaith venture largely in the historical-critical tradition, but originally designed with the "general reader" in mind. All Greek and Hebrew terms appear in transliteration. Each volume provides an extensive introduction followed, for each section of the biblical book, by: the author's own translation of the text; detailed notes on lexical, grammatical, and other interpretive issues; and extended commentary on the text. The *Anchor Bible* series has produced some superb, even classic, volumes but also some disasters (especially early on), which will probably be replaced. Apart from the few problem volumes, this series is highly respected among scholars. Each volume also includes a superb bibliography.

The *Augsburg Commentary on the New Testament* (Minneapolis: Augsburg, 1980–1990) is an excellent series devoted to literary and theological analysis with students and pastors in mind.

Berit Olam (Collegeville, Minn.: Liturgical, 1996–) is a series that takes a primarily literary approach to exegesis of the OT, with emphasis on the theological message of the text. The NRSV is the main English translation to which the commentators make reference.

Black's New Testament Commentaries (orig. New York: Harper, 1957–; now Peabody, Mass.: Hendrickson) is a venerable series, with selected volumes already replaced. The text is explained in blocks, with attention to historical, literary, and theological issues. This series was originally published as *Harper's New Testament Commentaries*.

The *Continental Commentary Series* (Philadelphia: Fortress and Minneapolis: Augsburg, 1984–) is a translation of European (mostly German) works with theological and literary as well as historical-critical interests. So far, more volumes have appeared on the OT than on the NT.

The *Hermeneia* series (Philadelphia/Minneapolis: Fortress, 1971–) is a classical historical-critical project inspired by German scholarship (in fact, some of the volumes are translations from German originals). Its strength is its attention to ancient sources and parallels to the biblical text and, more recently, to ancient rhetorical and literary features of the biblical books.

The International Critical Commentary series (Edinburgh: T&T Clark, 1896–) is a highly technical series that was first produced at the turn of the twentieth century and has been in the process of being redone, volume by volume, for several decades. Full of text and footnotes containing intricate discussions of grammar, the history of interpretation, nonbiblical literature, and related topics, these volumes— especially the recent ones—are invaluable for those who work in the original languages and useful even for those who do not.

The *International Theological Commentary* series (Grand Rapids: Eerdmans, 1983–) seeks to unpack the religious message of the text in short but insightful commentaries, each centering on a theme identified as central to the particular book under consideration. To date, only volumes on the OT have been issued.

Interpretation (Louisville: Westminster John Knox, 1982–) is an ecumenical series designed for "teaching and preaching." Although the series is somewhat uneven, it has produced a number of very fine commentaries. The goals of the series lead the commentators to focus on the final form of the text and on its significant literary and theological features. Many have notes on the use of their book in the lectionary, and most have specific sections devoted to theological reflection on the text.

The *New International Biblical Commentary* (Peabody, Mass.: Hendrickson, 1989–) is a very fine, very affordable paperback series prepared largely, though not exclusively, by well-known evangelical scholars. The text of the commentaries reproduces the biblical text of the NIV in boldface when it is quoted, and the endnotes for each section are especially good at conveying the history of interpretation and the variety of major contemporary interpretations of key aspects of the book. The NT is finished, and the OT is in the process of being completed.

The New International Commentary on the Old Testament (NICOT; Grand Rapids: Eerdmans, 1965–) and *The New International Commentary on the New Testament* (NICNT; Grand Rapids: Eerdmans, 1952–) are well-established, scholarly series prepared and edited by many of the major evangelical scholars of the last fifty years, with some of the older (and/or lesser) volumes now being replaced. The format is generally translation and notes plus verse-by-verse commentary. Newer volumes have sections on form and structure as well as theological reflection.

The *New International Greek Testament Commentary* (Grand Rapids: Eerdmans, 1978–) is a technical series on the Greek NT. The detailed, lengthy commentaries (several approaching or exceeding one thousand pages) pay close attention to linguistic and historical issues.

The NIV Application Commentary (Grand Rapids: Zondervan, 1994–), a series authored for the most part by reputable evangelical scholars, has as its primary goal "bringing an ancient message into a modern context." In addition to an introduction, outline, and bibliography, the commentary itself for each book contains three parts: the "Original Message," a section called "Bridging Contexts," and one called "Contemporary Significance." This approach is ambitious and creative, if at times a bit repetitious. On the whole, however, this series is rich in theological reflection and homiletical insight in the light of Western culture at the beginning of a new millennium.

The Old Testament Library (OTL) series (Philadelphia: Westminster and Louisville: Westminster John Knox, 1961–) brought critical German scholarship with literary and theological interests to the English-speaking world and now includes contributions from English-speaking scholars. In addition to commentaries, the series contains monographs on relevant topics. A New Testament counterpart (NTL) is soon to be published with original works in English.

The *Sacra Pagina* series (Collegeville, Minn.: Liturgical, 1991–) is an excellent collection of commentaries on the NT from well-known Roman Catholic biblical scholars. Original-language terms appear in transliteration. The format of each volume includes an introduction and passage-by-passage analysis, each with notes on every verse, a discussion of the passage as a whole, and a fine bibliography. These volumes are very sensitive to contemporary approaches and to theological significance.

The *Word Biblical Commentary* (WBC) series (Waco, Tex.: Word, 1983–) is a very thorough, technical, and highly respected series produced by some of the world's top evangelical scholars. Greek and Hebrew are used throughout. The format of each commentary includes an extensive introduction and then, for each passage: a bibliography; translation with textual notes; explanation of the "form/structure/setting"; verse-by-verse "comment"; and "explanation," which focuses on a synthesis of the meaning and function of the passage in context.

Multivolume Sets

Gaebelein, Frank, gen. ed. *The Expositor's Bible Commentary.* 12 vols. Grand Rapids: Zondervan, 1976–1992. This classic set by conservative evangelical scholars based on the NIV is responsible work but somewhat predictable in exegetical and theological perspective. It should therefore be used with some caution and balance from other perspectives. Available also on CD-ROM for both Windows and Macintosh.

The New Interpreter's Bible. 10 vols. to date. Nashville: Abingdon, 1994–. A monumental achievement, this twelve-volume set is replacing the old *Interpreter's Bible.* The scholarship is ecumenical and first-rate, the format attractive, and the connection between commentary and reflection superb. For each book of the Bible, including the apocryphal/deuterocanonical books, there is a substantial introduction preceding a unit-by-unit commentary and reflection. The entire text of both the NRSV and the NIV (excluding the Apocrypha) is printed, and there are charts and other aids. Many of the volumes contain general articles or articles introducing specific kinds of literature. An invaluable tool, indeed an instant classic. Also available on CD-ROM with powerful tools.

Section 7. Resources for Synthesis

As noted in the chapter itself, synthesis is an element of exegesis that can be accomplished only after giving careful attention to context, structure, and detail. Moreover, the individual and creative character of this element defies the production of simplistic "how-to" manuals for the synthetic dimension of exegesis.

Certain kinds of resources already discussed may, however, prove helpful. One-volume Bible commentaries, for instance, can be helpful in getting to the "punch line" of the text by virtue of their necessary brevity and, therefore (ideally) succinctness. But perhaps the most helpful resources for synthesis are more thorough commentaries that pay special attention either to the rhetorical features of the text, or to its theological claims, or (preferably) to both.

It is difficult to name particular commentary series that are uniformly useful in this regard, since the volumes in every series vary with respect to quality and insight. The *Interpretation* series is frequently helpful because of its attention to the theological dimensions of the text that can be preached and taught. Also, the *Word Biblical Commentary* and *Sacra Pagina* series, with their frequent attention to form and structure, may be worth consulting for this element of the exegetical process.

Section 8. Resources for Reflection

The following resources would normally appear in a bibliography entitled "hermeneutics." They represent diverse approaches to reading the text for its religious significance. As such, they are best read not in the "heat" of preparing an exegesis paper or sermon but at other times when more careful reflection on complex issues is possible. Of the many possible books that could be listed here, I have tried to select some that represent important recent trends.

Adam, A. K. M. *What Is Postmodern Biblical Criticism?* Guides to Biblical Scholarship. Minneapolis: Fortress, 1995. A brief, readable introduction to postmodernism and to deconstruction, political criticism, and related topics.

Braaten, Carl E., and Robert W. Jenson, eds. *Reclaiming the Bible for the Church.* Grand Rapids: Eerdmans, 1995. A collection of essays by an ecumenical group of biblical scholars and theologians who wish to use the historical approach to the Bible within the hermeneutical context of the entire canon and within the church's central faith convictions and practices.

Fowl, Stephen E. *Engaging Scripture: A Model for Theological Interpretation.* Challenges in Contemporary Theology. Oxford: Blackwell, 1998. A challenging and very significant argument that "Christians must read scripture in the light of their ends as Christians—ever deeper communion with the triune God and with each other," with examples of the model proposed.

————, ed. *The Theological Interpretation of Scripture: Classic and Contemporary Readers.* Oxford: Blackwell, 1997. A collection of significant essays from the past and present.

Fowl, Stephen E., and L. Gregory Jones. *Reading in Communion: Scripture and Ethics in Christian Life.* Grand Rapids: Eerdmans, 1991. Repr. Eugene, Ore.: Wipf and Stock, 1998. A masterful book on the nature of biblical interpretation as a communal practice of embodying Scripture within an ongoing interpretive tradition, with attention to interpreters and to specific texts.

González, Justo. *Santa Biblia: The Bible through Hispanic Eyes.* Nashville: Abingdon, 1996. Considers five paradigms for biblical interpretation (e.g., marginality, poverty) based on Latino experience.

Gottwald, Norman K., and Richard A. Horsley. *The Bible and Liberation: Political and Social Hermeneutics.* 2d ed. Maryknoll, N.Y.: Orbis, 1993. An impressive collection of more than thirty methodological and interpretive articles by leading proponents of these approaches to exegesis.

Green-McCreight, Kathryn, ed. *Theological Exegesis: Essays in Honor of Brevard S. Childs.* Grand Rapids: Eerdmans, 1998. A collection of essays from students, colleagues, and friends dedicated to further reflection on the "canonical criticism" that Childs espouses.

Hall, Christopher A. *Reading Scripture with the Church Fathers.* Downers Grove, Ill.: InterVarsity, 1998. A well-written introduction to the church fathers, their theological methods of exegesis, and especially their insistence on the role of community and character in appropriate biblical interpretation.

Hays, Richard B. **"Salvation by Trust? Reading the Bible Faithfully."** *Christian Century* 114 (Feb. 26, 1997): 218–23. A controversial article arguing for a hermeneutics of trust ("reading receptively and trustingly . . . but not accepting everything in the text at face value"), over against a hermeneutics of suspicion.

Lash, Nicholas. **"Performing the Scriptures."** Pages 37–46 in *Theology on the Way to Emmaus.* London: SCM, 1986. A classic essay on biblical interpretation as performance.

Levenson, Jon. *The Hebrew Bible, the Old Testament, and Historical Criticism.* Louisville: Westminster John Knox, 1993. A significant critique of the historical-critical method from a Jewish and interfaith perspective, with suggestions on more appropriate ways of reading the Bible.

Rowland, Christopher, and Mark Corner. *Liberating Exegesis: The Challenge of Liberation Theology to Biblical Studies.* Louisville: Westminster John Knox, 1989. A provocative discussion of various kinds of biblical study in Latin America and their possible impact on the study of the Bible in the "first world," with illustrations using NT texts.

Schüssler Fiorenza, Elisabeth, ed. *Searching the Scriptures.* Vol. 1. *A Feminist Introduction;* Vol. 2. *A Feminist Commentary.* New York: Crossroad, 1993, 1994. Feminist perspectives on biblical interpretation and texts, with an evaluation of traditional approaches.

Segovia, Fernando F., and Mary Ann Tolbert, eds. *Reading from This Place.* Vol. 1. *Biblical Interpretation and Social Location in the United States.* Vol. 2. *Biblical Interpretation and Social Location in the Global Scene.* Minneapolis: Fortress, 1995. Examples from a variety of locations of the importance of the human context in reading the Bible.

Stuhlmacher, Peter. *Historical Criticism and Theological Interpretation of Scripture.* Translated by Roy A. Harrisville. Philadelphia: Fortress, 1977. A brief, classic history and critique of changes in exegetical method since the time of early Christianity that separated faith from exegesis, and a defense of a "hermeneutics of consent" that includes "openness to transcendence."

Thiselton, Anthony. *New Horizons in Hermeneutics: The Theory and Practice of Transforming Biblical Reading.* Grand Rapids: Zondervan, 1992. A challenging, comprehensive review of hermeneutical approaches and their embodiment in actual biblical interpretation, together with Thiselton's own thesis, drawing upon speech-act theory, about the ways Bible reading can and should transform readers.

Watson, Francis. *Text, Church, and World: Biblical Interpretation in Theological Perspective.* Grand Rapids: Eerdmans, 1994. An important book arguing that "biblical interpretation should concern itself primarily with the theological issues raised by the biblical texts within our contemporary ecclesial, cultural, and socio-political concerns."

Wink, Walter. *The Bible in Human Transformation: Toward a New Paradigm for Biblical Study.* Philadelphia: Fortress, 1973. A small classic from the "existentialist" approach to exegesis.

Section 9. Bibliographical Resources

Exegetes have many resources at their disposal beyond those described in this book. Some books devoted to bibliography and some standard indexes to periodical literature are listed below. These may be used to locate books and articles on general or specific topics, and to supplement bibliographies found in or created from other kinds of resources.

BOOKS

Danker, Frederick W. *Multipurpose Tools for Bible Study.* Rev. and exp. ed. Minneapolis: Fortress, 1993. The latest edition of a classic first published in 1960, this book is a mine of information on the best resources of every type (concordances, editions and translations of the text, dictionaries, commentaries, etc.), advice on how best to use them, and examples of exegesis aided by the tools described. Mandatory repeated reading for serious students of the Bible.

Fitzmyer, Joseph A. *An Introductory Bibliography for the Study of Scripture.* 3d ed. Rome: Pontifical Biblical Institute, 1990. A regularly updated and helpful bibliography.

Hostetter, Edwin. *Old Testament Introduction.* IBR Bibliographies 11. Grand Rapids: Baker, 1995. An annotated bibliography of five hundred works on critical methods, ancient texts and versions, the language of the OT, cognate literature, and the "environment" (ancient world).

Porter, Stanley E., and Lee Martin McDonald. *New Testament Introduction.* IBR Bibliographies 12. Grand Rapids: Baker, 1995. An annotated bibliography of more than eight hundred works on language, exegesis and criticism, backgrounds, and introductory matters, including commentaries.

Powell, Mark Alan, ed. *The Bible and Modern Literary Criticism: A Critical Assessment and Annotated Bibliography.* New York: Greenwood, 1992. A very useful annotated bibliography of more than seventeen hundred books, articles, and other works on literary criticism of the Bible. Sections are devoted to theory and to method, but about one thousand of the entries are on specific books of the Bible, from Genesis to Revelation.

Watson, Duane F., and Alan J. Hauser. *Rhetorical Criticism of the Bible: A Comprehensive Bibliography with Notes on History and Method.* Leiden: Brill, 1994. A very helpful annotated bibliography on biblical rhetoric, organized according to biblical books, with notes on the history and theory of rhetorical criticism.

Zannoni, Arthur E. *The Old Testament: A Bibliography.* Collegeville, Minn.: Liturgical, 1992. A comprehensive but unannotated bibliography on texts and tools, exegetical methods, and specific books and texts.

PERIODICALS

Guides to periodicals are published in three forms: as bound volumes, as CD-ROMs, and as online databases. Among the most important are:

> ***New Testament Abstracts*** and ***Old Testament Abstracts.*** These two journals, published three times per year by the Catholic Biblical Association, provide short summaries, arranged by topic and book of the Bible, of recent scholarly articles. There are also notices of books published and reviewed. *Old Testament Abstracts* is available on CD-ROM.
>
> ***Religion Index One: Periodicals.*** This tool, published annually by the American Theological Library Association (ATLA), lists journal articles in all fields of theology and religious studies, including biblical studies. Articles on the Bible can be found arranged by topic, biblical writer, and biblical book.
>
> ***Religion Index Two: Multi-Author Works.*** This ATLA tool, parallel to *Religion Index One* in format, lists articles published in multi-author volumes (collections of essays).

The two indices from ATLA, part of the ATLA Religion Database (RDB), are available on CD-ROM and are in preparation for online access.

A Chart of Exegetical Methods

THREE APPROACHES

The following chart attempts to organize and display the various methods employed by practitioners of the synchronic, diachronic, and existential approaches to exegesis. For each method, the chart presents the phenomena or problems users of the method observe and seek to address; the goals of the method; and some sample questions that the method might generate.

The chart is not complete, for there are methods and "submethods" that could be added, but those included here are the main ones with which all exegetes should be familiar and which are discussed in this book. It should be remembered at all times that there is significant overlap between certain synchronic and diachronic methods and that the existential approach also makes use of methods from the other two approaches.

Method	Phenomena or Problems	Goals	Sample Questions
SYNCHRONIC **M**ETHODS (synchronic = within time) or Close Reading	A text is a finished product.	Analyze the text in its final form.	
Literary and Rhetorical Analysis			
Literary Criticism (including contextual analysis) Note: "literary criticism" is a rather vague term used in a variety of ways; see also narrative and rhetorical criticism below.	The meaning of texts is dependent on their nearer (or immediate) and larger contexts. Biblical documents exist as various kinds of literary works with corresponding features.	Determine contexts and their significance. Analyze various literary aspects of the text as literature.	What is the literary context of the so-called "suffering servant" hymn (Isaiah 53)? What kinds of figurative language are used in the book of Job? What are the dramatic features of the book of Revelation? Does Psalm 19 or John 1:1–18 have parallelism? inclusio? chiasm?
Genre and Form Analysis (genre = literary type or pattern) See also rhetorical criticism below and form criticism under diachronic methods.	Biblical writings contain various kinds of literary types.	Determine the genre or form of the text plus any key variations from normal patterns. Describe the structure and movement of the text (also part of rhetorical and literary criticism).	What type of psalm is Psalm 51? How is it arranged in verses (strophes)? What kind of writing is 1 Corinthians 13? How is 1 Corinthians 13 structured? Are there discernible parts?
Narrative Criticism	Many biblical writings contain, are based on, or are themselves explicit or implicit narratives (stories).	Analyze the text with respect to thematic lines, plot, character development, point of view, or other appropriate features of narratives.	What is the plot, and what are the key points in the sequence of events, in the Joseph cycle (Genesis 37–50)? How does Mark portray the disciples?

Method	Phenomena or Problems	Goals	Sample Questions
Rhetorical Criticism (rhetoric = the art of effective communication)	Texts exist to have an effect on the hearer/reader, and biblical writings exhibit ancient, modern, and universal rhetorical devices and forms.	Determine rhetorical strategies used (including tone, style) and their functions. Categorize text in terms of classical rhetorical forms. Describe the rhetorical structure of the text.	What is the rhetorical strategy and effect of God's speeches in Job? Of the kinds of persuasive writing known in antiquity, what kind is Galatians?
Linguistic Analysis			
Lexical, Grammatical, and Syntactical Analysis (vocabulary, forms of words, arrangement of words) See also historical linguistics below under diachronic methods.	Biblical writings contain significant and sometimes obscure words, grammatical forms, and syntactical constructions.	Determine the significance of key words, idioms Determine the significance of key grammatical forms. Determine the significance of key syntactical structures.	Is "Daughter Zion" or "Daughter of Zion" the best translation of the biblical phrase? If the Spirit is a "pledge" or "guarantee" (2 Corinthians 1:22), what did that mean in Paul's day? Does "love of Christ" (2 Corinthians 5:14) mean Christ's love or ours?
Semantic or Discourse Analysis (semantics = study of meaning)	Meaning is found not merely in the words and their forms and arrangements, but also in the contextual relations among them.	Use modern tools of linguistics to analyze the deep structure and other semantic features of discourse units.	How might contemporary understandings of the linguistic function of aphorisms assist in the interpretation of the book of Proverbs? What are the core affirmations in the phrase "[Jesus] was handed over to death for our trespasses and raised for our justification"?

Method	Phenomena or Problems	Goals	Sample Questions
Social-Scientific Criticism			
Social Description (general)	Biblical texts were produced in a concrete social and cultural situation. Biblical texts refer explicitly or implicitly to social customs, classes, conditions, relationships, etc.	Determine and describe the social context and cultural conditions of the writer and recipients. Describe the social world of the Israelites or early Christians.	In what changing social contexts did Jeremiah preach? What was the situation of the Johannine community? What evidence of patriarchal or elitist values can be found in the book of Proverbs? What was the socio-economic level of the first followers of Jesus, or of the Corinthian Christians?
Social-Scientific Analysis	Biblical writings may reflect realities that social sciences can explain.	Analyze the text or its community with sociological or anthropological models and methods.	Are there anthropological models or theories that help explain the rise of kingship in ancient Israel? Could belief in Jesus' resurrection be explained by the theory of "cognitive dissonance"?

Method	Phenomena or Problems	Goals	Sample Questions
DIACHRONIC **M**ETHODS (diachronic = across time) or Historical-Critical Method	A text has a history.	Discern and analyze the text's origin and development (and its final form in light of these).	
Textual Criticism	No "autographs" (originals) exist. Manuscripts and other witnesses disagree due to unintentional and intentional changes in the copying and transmission process.	Establish best text, as close to original as possible.	Did the original text say "only begotten God" or "only begotten Son" (John 1:18)? How does Mark's gospel end? Was the story of the woman caught in adultery originally part of John's gospel?
Historical Linguistics (vocabulary, forms of words, arrangement of words) See also lexical, grammatical, and syntactical analysis above under synchronic methods.	Biblical writings contain significant and sometimes obscure words, grammatical forms, and syntactical constructions, and these items have an important history.	See under "Synchronic Methods," plus . . . Determine the extent to which the historical development of these linguistic items is important for understanding the text.	See under "Synchronic Methods," plus . . . How do the histories of the words for "assembly" in the Bible develop over time and either reflect or affect writers' understandings of Israel or of the early house church?
Form Criticism (form = consistent pattern) See also genre and form analysis under synchronic methods.	Biblical writings contain various preliterary forms or patterns. These include, for example, proverbs, call stories, parables, beatitudes, healing stories, nature miracles, resurrection accounts, hymns, creeds, slogans, benedictions.	Determine the form of the text, plus any forms within it. Analyze any unusual features or changes to the form's normal pattern. Determine the original life setting *(Sitz im Leben)* in general for such a form.	What kind of narrative is the account of Moses and the burning bush (Exodus 3)? What kind of narrative is the story of Jesus and the disciples in the boat (Mark 4:35–41)? In what setting(s) of Israel's life or early Christianity would a certain kind of text (such as the two mentioned above) have been created and used, and why?

Method	Phenomena or Problems	Goals	Sample Questions
Tradition Criticism Note: this is a difficult and often speculative venture.	The oral tradition was modified in the transmission process.	Determine how a particular pericope came to be put together through a process of growth by oral transmission.	How was the story of the covenant promise to David (2 Samuel 7) modified as it was transmitted? Is the story of the paralytic man's being lowered and healed (Mark 2:1–12) a single story or a compilation of oral sources?
Source Criticism	Each writer appears to have used various sources to construct the finished product.	Determine the sources used, plus their types and perspectives.	What different sources were used to put together the two creation stories in Genesis 1–3? What was the nature of the material that Matthew and Luke have in common that is absent from Mark?
Redaction Criticism (redaction = editing; cf. also intertextuality = weaving in of other written documents)	Each writer both adopted and adapted sources, resulting in distinct perspectives.	Determine how the writer (or writing) uses (changes, does not change) sources; ask "why?" Trace tendencies, distinctive features, emphases, etc. in a document.	How has the editor of Exodus combined and edited sources about Moses, and for what purposes? How does Matthew both adopt and adapt Mark's account of Jesus' baptism, and why?

Method	Phenomena or Problems	Goals	Sample Questions
Historical Criticism	Biblical preliterary forms and actual texts were produced in concrete historical situations. Because the oral tradition was modified in the transmission and redaction process, it may be that not every word and deed reflected in the biblical text actually occurred. Other things claimed in the biblical writings may or may not have happened as presented.	Determine the historical contexts reflected in preliterary forms and in the written text. Determine what, if anything, a historical figure actually said and did, and what was modified and/or created by the process of tradition and redaction.	What if anything can be known of the actual experience of the figure Abraham? How does one account for the parting of the Red/Reed Sea in historical and scientific terms? What was the occasion for the writing of Habakkuk? Do the accounts of Jesus' conflict with the Pharisees correspond to his actual conflicts, those of the evangelists' time, or both? Did Jesus predict his own suffering, death, and resurrection, or did the early church put those words on his lips?

Method	Phenomena or Problems	Goals	Sample Questions
EXISTENTIAL METHODS (existential = concerning real life)	A biblical text makes claims on and speaks to later readers, but there is a wide historical and cultural gap between the time of writing and today.	Discern the contemporary meaning of the text by using synchronic and diachronic approaches mixed with additional methods, theories, and contexts.	
Hermeneutics of Trust or Consent			
Canonical Criticism	From the believing community's perspective, biblical texts and documents exist not alone but as part of a larger collection, the canon.	Determine meaning and authority of texts in their relationship with other similar and dissimilar texts.	How do we understand the nature of God portrayed in the books of Hosea and Amos in light of the entire canon? How do Paul's emphasis on justification through faith and James's stress on good works illumine each another?
Theological Exegesis	Ultimately, the Bible speaks about Jewish and Christian theological convictions.	Discern the authoritative theological and ethical claims of the text.	To what way of life does the prophet Jeremiah point us? What do the images of the book of Revelation say to Christians about God and Christ?
Spiritual Reading (*Lectio Divina* or praying scripture, and "reading in communion")	Ultimately, Scripture, as the word of God, is not something to dissect but to hear and respond to as divine address to individuals and communities.	Discern the specific word of God being addressed to me or us.	How does Psalm 150 express and nurture our life of praise? What does the story of Peter's denial say to us? How might we be denying our Lord?

Method	Phenomena or Problems	Goals	Sample Questions
Embodiment or Actualization (praxis, performance, living exegesis)	Ultimately, Scripture is not something merely to study but to live.	Embody the claims, promises, and imperatives of the text as a faithful person and community.	How are we to identify and treat the "orphan and the widow" in our midst? What are we specifically to do to embody the concern for the marginalized and outcast that Jesus exhibits in Luke?
Hermeneutics of Suspicion			
Advocacy and Liberationist Exegesis (includes feminist and other liberationist perspectives)	Biblical writings have been interpreted in ways that offend or oppress (anti-Semitism, slavery, gender discrimination, etc.). Biblical writings may themselves contain things deemed, by some, to be offensive or oppressive.	Determine how the Bible has been used to oppress, and use specific texts to stress its nonoppressive, liberating meaning. Consider or determine which texts and themes may need to be avoided, which used, in order to advocate and work for liberation.	How have people used the Bible to justify discrimination against women? Is the Gospel of John so inherently anti-Semitic that its presence in the Christian New Testament is problematic?
Ideological Criticism	Biblical writings may reflect and support inappropriate expressions of power.	Determine and critique the inappropriate relations of power.	To what appropriate and inappropriate relations of economic power does the wisdom literature bear witness? Does Paul's eschatology in 1 Corinthians 7 implicitly approve of the powerful keeping the powerless in a subservient position?

Practical Guidelines for Writing a Research Exegesis Paper

There are five major phases in the writing of a research exegesis paper: preparation, initial exegesis, research, consolidation, and writing.

I. Preparation

    A. Determine an appropriate text for exegesis: a manageable, relatively self-contained unit with a clear beginning and end. (chapter 2)

        1. The length should normally be no less than the equivalent of a paragraph or stanza and no more than the equivalent of a few paragraphs or stanzas (e.g., approximately five to twenty-five verses).

        2. Study Bibles or one-volume commentaries may be helpful in determining units.

        3. Consult with your instructor for advice if necessary.

    B. Obtain the biblical texts with which you plan to work—a study Bible, one or more additional translations, editions with parallel texts (e.g., gospel parallels, if appropriate), and the Greek or Hebrew text (if you read it).

    C. Photocopy from a Bible, or print from an electronic version, at least one version of your text for the purpose of marking it up.

        1. Place the text in the center of the page, with wide margins on either side. If possible, import the text into a word processor and print it out with wide spacing between the lines of text.

2. If possible, also create with the word-processor a two-column phrase-by-phrase chart of the text for use in the detailed analysis.

II. Initial Exegesis

Note: Work on the text on your own, writing down whatever you discover, and whatever questions come to mind, as you follow the main steps of the exegetical process. Mark up your photocopy of the text: underline, circle, make notes, etc. Note any specific questions that you wish to research in the commentaries, books, and articles you will use in the next phase, expansion and refinement of the exegesis. You may wish to organize your observations on note cards or on pieces of paper dedicated to the various elements (with separate cards or sheets for each verse examined in the detailed analysis).

A. Survey: The First Element (chapter 3)
  1. Read the text several times and in several translations.
      a. Write down first observations, key differences in the translations, and questions that arise.
      b. Make an initial working translation of the text, if you read the original language.
  2. Read or skim the entire book in which the text appears, paying special attention to the text before and after your passage.
  3. Consult one or more resources that deal with the book in which the passage is located (introductory text, one-volume commentary, or Bible dictionary), and take notes on what you discover about:
      a. the basic historical context—the circumstances of its writing (who, what, when, why, where, etc.); and
      b. the basic literary context—a general outline of the book and the location of the passage in that outline.
  4. Begin to prepare a bibliography by noting any relevant commentaries, books, or articles mentioned in the resources consulted.
  5. Make an educated guess about the meaning of the passage, and use this as a working thesis.

B. Contextual Analysis: The Second Element (chapter 4)
  1. Historical, Social, and Cultural Contexts—Use a Bible dictionary or similar resource to obtain basic information as necessary.

2. Literary and Rhetorical Context
    a. Find or create a general outline of the book as a whole.
    b. Carefully consider the wider as well as nearer or immediate context.

C. Formal Analysis: The Third Element (chapter 5)
The Form, Structure, and Movement of the Passage
    1. Form—Consider the literary genre of the book and the literary form of the passage.
    2. Structure—Create your own outline of the passage.
    3. Movement—Consider how the text flows from beginning to end.

D. Detailed Analysis: The Fourth Element (chapter 6)
Verse-By-Verse Discussion
    1. Use the two-column, phrase-by-phrase chart created during the preparation phase.
    2. Find key actors and actions (subjects, verbs, etc.), qualifying phrases, other key words and images, etc.
    3. Pay special attention to function words (because, for, although, when, if, etc.).
    4. Look for allusions to other texts, especially Scripture, and for evidence of other sources and how they are used.

E. Synthesis: The Fifth Element (chapter 7)
Formulate the main point of the text.

F. Reflection: The Sixth Element (chapter 8)
Make observations about the contemporary significance of the text from your perspective.

III. Research: The Seventh Element (chapter 9)
Expansion and Refinement of Your Initial Exegesis

A. Prepare a bibliography.
    1. Use note cards or a list, making sure the information is complete.
    2. Types of resources: reference books (Bible dictionaries and the like); monographs that discuss your passage; commentaries on the book; periodical articles; chapters in volumes of collected essays.
    3. How to find resources: read bibliographies and notes in textbooks, commentaries, reference books, study Bibles, etc.; use bibliographical tools; browse the card catalog, books in the stacks, and current periodicals.

4. Length of bibliography—rule of thumb: approximately one bibliographical item for each page of text (e.g., a fifteen-page paper should have about fifteen bibliographical entries).

B. Take careful notes.
1. Use commentaries before articles (general to specific).
2. Look for information, insights, and interpretations that escaped your initial exegesis.
3. Look to challenge, clarify, and correct your own work.
4. Look for and record evidence of the important aspects of the text.
5. Look for alternative interpretations of important issues and document them.
6. Generally, take notes in your own words; put direct quotes in quotation marks.

C. Review your notes.
1. Look for any gaps in data or interpretation.
2. Reuse resources or find new resources as necessary.

IV. Consolidation: The Seventh Element (chapter 9)
Expansion and Refinement of Your Initial Exegesis (continued)

A. Combine your initial exegesis with the corrections, confirmations, new data and evidence, etc. from other sources.

B. Write down your own conclusions and claims about the context, form/structure/movement, main aspects (including debated points) of the detailed analysis, and synthesis.

C. Develop and record a thesis statement about the main point(s) and function of the passage.

D. Develop an outline of your paper that follows the main steps in the exegetical process.

V. Writing

A. Start with the contexts, then form/structure/movement. Do detailed analysis and synthesis next, and the introduction to the paper last (unless you are to include a section of personal reflection and engagement, which may be written last).

B. Note that "refinement and expansion of the exegesis" is not a separate section of the paper, only a stage in the process.

C. Discuss and evaluate the most important alternative interpretations of the most important issues, but do not create a collage of book reports or a review of research. Constantly and consistently state and defend your informed interpretation of the text.

D. Document—in parentheses, endnotes, or footnotes—information, insights, and interpretations discovered in your research.

E. Follow the form for papers outlined in the standard guide to paper writing used in your institution.

F. Reread, rewrite, reread, rewrite.

A Short Sample Exegesis Paper

The following short exegesis paper was written at about the midway point in a course on the Gospel of John. The author was a part-time student in an M.A. in Theology program and does not read Greek, working instead with the NRSV. The only sources she consulted for the paper were the textbooks for this course and for another class in Christian origins. This fine essay appears unedited except for minor adjustments to its format.

An Exegesis of John 11:45–53
Annette Chappell

45Many of the Jews therefore, who had come with Mary and had seen what Jesus did, believed in him. 46But some of them went to the Pharisees and told them what he had done. 47So the chief priests and the Pharisees called a meeting of the council, and said, "What are we to do? This man is performing many signs. 48If we let him go on like this, everyone will believe in him, and the Romans will come and destroy both our holy place and our nation." 49But one of them, Caiaphas, who was high priest that year, said to them, "You know nothing at all! 50You do not understand that it is better for you to have one man die for the people than to have the whole nation destroyed." 51He did not say this on his own, but being high priest that year he prophesied that Jesus was about to die for the nation, 52and not for the nation only, but to gather into one the dispersed children of God. 53So from that day on they planned to put him to death. (NRSV)

John 11:45–53 presents the plotting of the Jewish council in a way that reinforces several Johannine themes, especially the divided responses of the people to Jesus; the increasing hostility of the Jewish leadership to Jesus; the irony of that hostility in the face of God's unshakable plan; and the divine necessity of the crucifixion as the "completion" of Jesus' career on earth.

HISTORICAL CONTEXT

In interpreting this pericope it is particularly important to understand the delicate and precarious relationship of the Jewish authorities with their Roman overlords. The deliberations of the Jewish council reveal not only a (perhaps self-serving) concern with preserving the leadership the Romans have permitted them to exercise, but also a probably quite legitimate fear that any activity that upsets the Roman authorities can only result in repression of both the Jewish religion and the Jewish people.

LITERARY CONTEXT

This passage occurs near the end of the first half of the gospel of John (the "Book of Signs"), just after the raising of Lazarus from the dead. The raising of Lazarus is the most dramatic, and the most clearly eschatological, of Jesus' signs. That incident is his last "public appearance" before the events we associate with Holy Week (the triumphal entry into Jerusalem and all that follows). John 11:45–53 therefore provides both a bridge between major sections of the narrative and a distillation of the evangelist's understanding of the causes (human and divine so ironically blended) of the trial and crucifixion.

FORM, STRUCTURE, MOVEMENT

This pericope provides both a conclusion to the Lazarus story and a transition to the increasingly tense events of Jesus' final week on earth. Not only does the passage foreshadow the crucifixion in general ("they planned to put him to death," v. 53), but also it hints at the complex manipulations the Jewish authorities will use to persuade their Roman overlords to order and carry out that execution.

The pericope is structured as an extended dialogue, a series of implicit and explicit speeches illustrating the sequence of reactions to Jesus' raising of Lazarus from the dead. The discussion moves from the most public level, where the reaction of bystanders is divided (vv. 45–46), to the inner circles of Jewish leadership, where the event is seen as the latest in a sequence of increasingly objectionable actions by Jesus (vv. 47–50 and vv. 51–52), and where the resolve to eliminate Jesus seems the only appropriate conclusion for the council to reach (v. 53).

DETAILED ANALYSIS

In 11:45–46, as on so many occasions in the fourth gospel, the reaction to Jesus' act is decidedly mixed. Raising Lazarus from the dead is the most extraordinary act Jesus has yet performed in this gospel, both because it so far transcends the ordinary laws of nature and because Jesus so explicitly uses the prayer at 11:41–42 as a teaching tool. However, though "many" believe in him as a result, there are "some" who instead go to the Pharisees and bear witness against Jesus. Their witness-bearing is reported, not dramatized as quotation; we can assume, however, that it is not deliberate "false witness" (as in Mark and Matthew), but is nevertheless wrong because those who go to the Pharisees have failed to understand who Jesus is.

The segment 11:47–50 presents a dramatic scene, in which the Jewish authorities articulate the political fears that Jesus' activities evoke. The problem, as it is expressed by the "chief priests and Pharisees" in vv. 47–49, is that Jesus' popularity with the (Jewish) crowds may draw the attention of the Romans to the Jewish nation as a whole. In their estimation, the Romans will assume that Jesus' popularity presages a nationalistic uprising, and in order to forestall such an uprising the Romans will suppress the Jewish religion ("destroy . . . our holy place" in v. 48 may mean physically destroy the Temple and certainly means suppress the system of worship that takes place there), which will lead to destruction of the Jewish "nation," since the only national identity the Jews had left under Roman rule was their devotion to Temple and Torah.

Commentators note that the fourth evangelist was imprecise in characterizing the members of the council (Kysar, 184), using the term "Pharisees" in a manner appropriate to his own time rather than to Jesus' time. The implication, however, is clear: the council is made up of religious leaders ("chief priests and Pharisees") for whom Jesus poses a threat both to their own status and to their religion and nation.

The high priest, Caiaphas, however, suggests that the solution is quite simple (11:49–50): Jesus must "die for the people" so that the whole nation will not be destroyed. From this clear insight, the plot against Jesus can easily be developed.

The literary focus of the entire pericope is on the layers of irony implicit in Caiaphas's pronouncement. Though there may be historical interest in the question of whether 11:51 indicates a general belief that being high priest conveyed the ability to prophesy (Kysar, 186; Talbert, 177; *Harper-Collins Study Bible,* 2037 f.n.), the main function of vv. 51–52 is to call the reader's attention to the complex irony.

In this passage, at least the following levels of irony are operating all at once: (1) Caiaphas and the rest of the council believe they are opposing Jesus and thwarting his mission, when in fact they are instrumental in precipitating the crucifixion, which is precisely the "completion" toward which Jesus' ministry must move. (2) Caiaphas believes he is smarter than the rest of the council because he alone has discovered how to get rid of Jesus, when in fact he is as oblivious to the truth as the rest of the council. (3) Caiaphas and the council conclude that Jesus' death will save "the whole nation" from the Romans, whereas in fact, his death will save not only the nation of Israel but also "the dispersed children of God," including the Romans and other pagans the council so fears. (4) Caiaphas and the council believe they are protecting the Temple and its cultus from destruction at Roman hands, though the evangelist and his readers know that the Romans did destroy the Temple in 70 C.E. and with it the social/ecclesiastical/liturgical structure it supported. (5) Caiaphas and the council are concerned to protect Judaism from pagan gentiles, the Romans, but since Jesus' death will be "not for the nation only, but to gather together the dispersed children of God," including all those gentiles, the result will be Christian communities such as John's that exemplify that multiculturalism and make the council's brand of accommodationist Judaism obsolete. (6) The chief servants of YHWH, God's representatives to the people, are convinced that for the sake of the people they need to procure the death of God's prophet, God's Son, God's Logos, God's own self, because they deny that that is who they are condemning. (7) In fact, for God's own purposes, it is necessary that the Son should die; the council unwittingly participates in bringing about that completion of God's plan for the nation of Israel and "the dispersed children of God."

The pericope ends with the council's resolve (11:53) to find a way to put Jesus to death. As we know from ch. 12, they eventually conclude that they will also need to kill Lazarus, who is visibly a beneficiary of Jesus' divine power. The final irony of this passage, then, is that Caiaphas and the council have totally miscalculated the nature of *witness*. In addition to thinking of Lazarus as no more than an inconvenient piece of evidence, they assume that the people will no longer be witnesses once Jesus is dead. As the evangelist has made increasingly clear in this gospel, however, *witness* is a result of *belief*, and once people truly believe in Jesus, they do not cease to witness to him. This passage therefore leads into the second half of John's gospel, the "Book of Glory," the story of Jesus' last days on earth and his exaltation as Son of God on the cross.

SYNTHESIS/CONCLUSION

Through the dramatic little story of the council's discussion after the raising of Lazarus, the fourth evangelist accomplishes several purposes. He creates a transition from the last great sign story, the raising of Lazarus, to the beginning of the story of Jesus' last days. In so doing, he heightens the tension as Jesus is more and more in danger from the authorities. He reminds his audience of the divided response all Jesus' actions evoked from the people, and of the implacable opposition of the Jewish authorities. He uses complex irony to indict the Jewish leadership for their misunderstanding of Jesus, of God, and of God's plan for the world. And he reinforces the sense of inevitability with which his narrative builds toward the crucifixion as the moment when Christ is "raised up" as lord and savior.

REFLECTION

In the context of his own apologetic, the fourth evangelist seems inclined to make the Jewish authorities into deliberately malevolent antagonists. After all, for him they "represent" the later synagogue authorities who expelled the Johannine Christians from synagogue fellowship and worship. The author's artistry, however, is more generous than he perhaps knew, and his irony in this little scene transcends his antipathy toward the Jewish leaders. Thus, although there is certainly no sweetness in John's treatment of the "chief priests and Pharisees," they do come through as confused but perhaps not evil human beings, caught up in something they could neither understand nor ignore, and addressing a new problem with the wrong old ways of reasoning. Alas, the church today is not immune to that kind of mistake, so it should be a comfort to be reminded that God's gracious irony can make our bumbling errors part of God's great plan.

WORKS CONSULTED

Ferguson, Everett. *Backgrounds of Early Christianity.* 2d ed. Grand Rapids: Eerdmans, 1993.

Kysar, Robert. *John.* Augsburg Commentary on the New Testament. Minneapolis: Augsburg, 1986.

Meeks, Wayne, et al., eds. *The HarperCollins Study Bible, NRSV with the Apocryphal/Deuterocanonical Books.* New York: HarperCollins, 1993.

Talbert, Charles H. *Reading John: A Literary and Theological Commentary on the Fourth Gospel and the Johannine Epistles.* New York: Crossroad, 1992.

A Longer Sample Exegesis Paper

The exegesis paper on the following pages was written toward the end of a course on the Pauline Epistles. The author was a full-time student in an M.Div. program, preparing for priesthood in the Roman Catholic Church. At the time of the course, he was in the beginning of his second of four years in the program. His paper is based largely on the NAB, with reference to the NRSV and some Greek, which he does not know well. This paper was intended to include research in the secondary literature and to include footnotes. This very good essay appears unedited except for minor technical adjustments.

Weakness as an Apostolic Credential: 2 Corinthians 12:1–10
Bryan Lowe

[1] I must boast; not that it is profitable, but I will go on to visions and revelations of the Lord. [2] I know someone in Christ who, fourteen years ago (whether in the body or out of the body I do not know, God knows), was caught up to the third heaven. [3] And I know that this person (whether in the body or out of the body I do not know, God knows) [4] was caught up into Paradise and heard ineffable things, which no one may utter. [5] About this person I will boast, but about myself I will not boast, except about my weaknesses. [6] Although if I should wish to boast, I would not be foolish, for I would be telling the truth. But I refrain, so that no one may think more of me than what he sees in me or hears from me [7] because of the abundance of the revelations. Therefore, that I might not become too elated, a thorn in the flesh was given to me, an

angel of Satan, to beat me, to keep me from being too elated. [8] Three times I begged the Lord about this, that it might leave me, [9] but he said to me, "My grace is sufficient for you, for power is made perfect in weakness." I will rather boast most gladly of my weaknesses, in order that the power of Christ may dwell with me. [10] Therefore, I am content with weaknesses, insults, hardships, persecutions, and constraints, for the sake of Christ; for when I am weak, then I am strong. (NAB)

Paul's Second Letter to the Corinthians is not one of the more well-known Pauline texts. Although there has been much debate about the literary integrity of the letter, there is little doubt that the letter was originally circulated in its present canonical form. The passage to be analyzed, 2 Corinthians 12:1–10, is an interesting one for many reasons. In it we have Paul's first hand (though narrated in the third person) account of his vision of Paradise. Although by most people's standards this would certainly give Paul something to "brag about," Paul's reason for including it is specifically to show that boasting is not what being an apostle is all about. Paul is providing a polemical argument against so-called "super-apostles" in Corinth who seem to be trying to supplement his teaching with a different gospel.

In the larger context of Paul's argument, weakness is a main theme. Paul uses the phrase often within this passage as well, with "weak" or "weakness" occurring five times. This weakness is a focus for Paul in the apostolic life. In conforming oneself more closely to Christ and living the "cruciform" lifestyle Paul expounds, one will be less self-reliant, and thus God's power can be displayed for all to see.

Paul's argument provides us with more than just a glimpse at what his opponents at Corinth were claiming. This passage gives a clearer understanding of Paul's vision of apostolic ministry in general. Phrases such as "my grace is sufficient for you" and "when I am weak, then I am strong" are well known to most people who have even a limited acquaintance with Scripture. In analyzing Paul's argument in 2 Corinthians 12:1–10, these statements take on a new, more sophisticated meaning.

HISTORICAL AND LITERARY CONTEXTS

Paul was the founder of the Christian community at Corinth. It appears that he initially stayed there for approximately eighteen months. Paul apparently wrote a series of letters to the Corinthians in his ongoing attempt to be an absentee pastor to a community that obviously meant a great deal to him. As Mary Ann Getty describes the situation:

> The letters we call 1 and 2 Corinthians formed a part of a larger collection that originally consisted of several letters Paul wrote to the Corinthian community. Paul's relationship with the Corinthians was complex and tumultuous and it seems as if the Corinthians were a particularly challenging community.[1]

This would seem to be an understatement, to say the least. The issue of allegiance to Paul as opposed to others was apparent in 1 Corinthians, and the same sort of issue is again revisited in 2 Corinthians. The most that I feel can be said with confidence is that Paul had to deal with a number of issues with respect to the Corinthians, among them being his status as an apostle.

There has been a great deal of speculation in regard to the literary integrity of 2 Corinthians, as well as in regard to the date it was written. The biggest source of controversy seems to be 2 Corinthians 10–13. While there are other parts of this letter that are also considered to be insertions (some claim up to five different letters), the focus of this section will be on chs. 10 to 13. These four chapters are obviously an integral literary unit unto themselves. The disagreement comes in determining whether these chapters were originally part of the letter or were combined with chs. 1–9 by a later redactor. The point of contention comes in the seemingly abrupt change of tone from 9:15 to 10:1. Many commentators (so Martin, Murphy-O'Connor, and Furnish) see this change as so drastic that chs. 10–13 must be a separate letter, or at least a part of a separate letter.

---

[1] Mary Ann Getty, "Paul and His Writings," in Donald Senior, ed., *The Catholic Study Bible* (New York: Oxford University Press, 1990), RG [reading guide] 485.

On the other hand, I believe that the themes are so consistent throughout the entirety of 2 Corinthians, that the entire letter must be viewed as a whole. Throughout the early parts of the letter Paul refers to problems in the community and to an upcoming visit. This seems to lay the groundwork for chs. 10–13. His discussion of "letters of recommendation" in 3:1 could be seen as a beginning of his discussion that is completed in the later chapters. The discussion of an upcoming visit in ch. 7 is echoed in chs. 10–13. Linda Belleville states that this "visit talk" is what ties ch. 7 to 13 together.[2] Paul's discussion of his ministry in 4:7–18 certainly seems to be summed up with "when I am weak, then I am strong" in 12:10b. The continuity of themes expressed between the various parts of the letter are sufficient to convince me that the canonical form of 2 Corinthians was originally sent as an intact letter, but, as Raymond Brown states, "surety is not obtainable."[3]

As far as date written, most commentators choose a date sometime in 55 for ch. 1–9 (or for the entire letter for the minority who agree with my opinion), with chs. 10–13 being written a few months later.[4] The place of composition is generally assumed to be Macedonia. Based on Paul's mention of a third visit, it seems likely that the visit would have been sometime in late 55 or 56.

In the larger literary context, 2 Cor 12:1–10 is a part of the unit of ch. 10–13 as discussed above. Paul devotes this entire section to a vigorous defense of his ministry and his apostolic credentials. The unity of this section can be particularly seen in the fact that Paul's "trials-list" occurs midway through the section. "The centrality of this 'trials-list'

---

[2] Linda L. Belleville, *2 Corinthians.* IVP New Testament Commentary Series, vol. 8 (Downers Grove, Ill.: InterVarsity, 1996), 21.

[3] Raymond E. Brown, *An Introduction to the New Testament* (New York: Doubleday, 1997), 551.

[4] See the works by Belleville, Brown, Furnish, Martin, and Murphy-O'Connor for more detailed discussions of the dating of this letter and of Paul's visits to Corinth.

within chaps. 10–13 is also a literal one, since 11:21b–29 occurs exactly in the middle of this last section of the letter."[5] This centrality of Paul's sufferings is key for his argument that apostleship is not about physical appearance. As Jerry Sumney writes:

> Explicit statements in chs. 10–13 show that the *central issue* at Corinth *is the appropriate way of life* for apostles. The opponents contend that true apostles should be impressive individuals. They should be dynamic and persuasive speakers and have a commanding demeanor. This impressive way of life includes the power to rise above troubles.[6]

In the nearer literary context, 2 Corinthians 12: 1–10 is a part of the so-called "Fool's Speech" that runs from 11:1 to 12:13.[7] Paul is taking on his opponents by using their own methods, and he begs the Corinthians to "put up with a little foolishness" (11:1) from him. He is apparently using some of his opponents' arguments against them in the speech, although it is difficult to be certain. The question of who Paul's opponents are in this section also needs to be discussed briefly. From looking at Paul's discussion of the two covenants in 2 Corinthians 3 it seems possible that Paul was dealing with a group of Hellenistic "Judaizers" who valued personal charism in preaching while attempting to supplement Paul's teaching with the Mosaic law.

FORM, STRUCTURE, AND MOVEMENT

Paul's Second Letter to the Corinthians is obviously in the form of a letter. When viewed as a whole, the entire structure of canonical 2 Corinthians seems to follow Paul's

---

[5] Michael L. Barré, "Qumran and the 'Weakness' of Paul," *Catholic Biblical Quarterly* 42 (1980): 216.

[6] Jerry L. Sumney, *Identifying Paul's Opponents: The Question of Method in 2 Corinthians*. Journal for the Study of the New Testament Supplement Series, vol. 40 (Sheffield, England: JSOT Press, 1990), 162.

[7] Jerome Murphy-O'Connor, *The Theology of the Second Letter to the Corinthians*. New Testament Theology (Cambridge, England: Cambridge University Press, 1991), 107.

"typical A-B-A' pattern that influenced so heavily the development of 1 Corinthians": chs. 1–7 are a discussion of difficulties at Corinth (A), chs. 8–9 are a discussion of successes seen at Corinth (B), and chs. 10–13 are a return to difficulties (A').[8] Second Corinthians 12: 1–10 is a polemical argument within his larger argument of chs. 10–13 concerning apostolic authority.[9] In this section he addresses his opponents using their own understanding of what constitutes apostolic authority. As Ralph Martin summarizes:

> In 12:1–10, we have a mosaic of literary devices that yields an interesting picture. In this passage Paul is answering a criticism from his opponents, namely, that he boasts little, and even when he boasts, it is only of weakness. Paul's reply is to engage in an *ad hominem* argument. He will presently meet the opponents on their own level and then, in a masterful way, show that it is his ministry, not theirs, that is of God.[10]

For the sake of discussion, this passage can be divided into five separate parts. These divisions, while somewhat arbitrary, are based on thematic changes in the passage as much as on content. The divisions are as follows:

a) Introduction—the need for boasting (v. 1)

b) Paul's "visions and revelations" (vv. 2–4)

c) Return to boasting (vv. 5–7a)

d) Paul's "thorn in the flesh" (vv. 7b–9a)

e) Final boasting of weakness (vv. 9b–10)

DETAILED ANALYSIS

Introduction—the need for boasting (v. 1)

Paul begins this section by apparently meeting his opponents on their own terms. His statement that "I must (or "it

---

[8] The quotation and the designation of the various sections come from Getty, "Writings," RG 496.

[9] Ralph P. Martin, *2 Corinthians*. Word Biblical Commentary, vol. 40 (Waco, Tex.: Word, 1986), 390–91.

[10] Ibid., 390.

is necessary to," NRSV) boast" seems to be a concession to his opponents that if he is to argue against them he must do so in the same way they have argued against him. However, Paul immediately makes the point that his boasting will not be profitable (or, it will do no good). It seems likely that his opponents must have been making claims of their own ecstatic experiences, and "the value that the early church placed on such experiences can be seen from the fact that Paul in his boasting turns last to *visions and revelations*."[11] Paul has already in 11:17 described his "boastful state" as "foolishness," and he obviously sees no gain in boasting of anything other than his weaknesses, which he previously described in 11:21b–29. Therefore, this final boasting on Paul's part is apparently meant to address the claims that his opponents are making. In the words of Victor Furnish:

> Paul will support his apostleship only by boasting of his weaknesses (11:30; 12:5, 9–10): while he is willing to record this one instance of a private religious experience, he is quite unwilling to claim it as an apostolic credential.[12]

Paul's "visions and revelations" (vv. 2–4)

The structure of Paul's description of his "visions and revelations" is unusual, to say the least. The immediate questions that come to mind are:

a) Why does he use the third person to describe the experience?

b) What is the significance of the date "fourteen years ago"?

c) Why does he use an apparently redundant structure in recounting the experience?

I will address each of these questions individually.

---

[11] Belleville, *2 Corinthians*, 299.

[12] Victor Paul Furnish, *II Corinthians: Translation, Introduction, Notes and Commentary*. Anchor Bible, vol. 32A (New York: Doubleday, 1984), 544.

a) Many possibilities have been offered to explain Paul's use of the third person rather than the first person in his account. At first glance, it seems likely that Paul is simply trying to distance himself from the description since he does not intend to boast about it. However, on further reflection, I believe that Victor Furnish offers the most probable reason. He believes that Paul was following in the convention used in other ancient accounts of heavenly journeys. The use of the third person then becomes a kind of "self-transcendence" from which to narrate the story.[13] This seems to make the most sense, because it is clear from the context of the argument as a whole that Paul is describing something that happened to him personally.

b) The date of "fourteen years ago" seems very important to Paul in describing his experience. It is probable that tying the ecstatic experience to an exact date is the only way Paul can validate his experience. This would be particularly true since he cannot discuss what he heard. It is also likely that the date must have been significant for Paul personally. "When it comes to such a landmark experience he has the exact date well in mind."[14]

c) The structure of Paul's narrative is the most puzzling aspect of this section because of the way that v. 2 seems to be paralleled by vv. 3–4. The most common question would be whether Paul is describing a single journey or two journeys. Once again it seems unlikely that this is a description of two separate journeys. It is possible that Paul was using the parallel structure to highlight the importance of the event, but this does not seem like a technique that he has employed before. It would then appear to be redundant simply for the sake of being redundant. The most plausible explanation is offered by James Tabor, and explains the journey as a single one completed in two stages:

---

[13] Ibid., 543.

[14] James D. Tabor, *Things Unutterable: Paul's Ascent to Paradise in Its Greco-Roman, Judaic, and Early Christian Contexts.* Studies in Judaism (Lanham, Md.: University Press of America, 1986), 115.

Paradise is the goal of the journey, and it is the highest goal one could claim, something one could call "extraordinary," and over which one could easily become elated (2 Cor. 12:7). He reports it in a two stage journey, which accounts for the parallel structure. He has been to the third heaven, yes, but beyond that, he has entered Paradise. And it is there, in Paradise, before God's throne, that he hears things unutterable. This interpretation seems to best fit the structure and content of the report.[15]

In this scenario, the "third heaven" would be the first stage of Paul's journey, which is also a destination his opponents might have been claiming. The second stage of the trip— "Paradise"—would be much more remarkable because it would necessarily entail some kind of direct contact with God. This is where he heard unutterable things. "Significantly, and in striking contrast to other ancient accounts of such journeys, the apostle has nothing to say about what he saw in Paradise."[16] This difference between Paul's report and traditional reports would certainly seem to be intended to place his journey in a higher category than those of his opponents. Paul's statements about not knowing whether his journey was in or out of the body are seemingly of little consequence to his description. They seem merely to be statements of fact that he is not certain how the journey was accomplished, except that he was "caught up." His avoidance of any attempt to understand how this happened could fit well with his desire for his opponents to see this as a factual account and not an interpretation of his journey.

Return to boasting (vv. 5–7a)

Having described his experience in Paradise, Paul returns once again to the subject of boasting. The irony of Paul's account is that an actual encounter with God would seem to be something worth boasting about, but Paul refuses to boast, except about his weaknesses. In this section it becomes apparent that Paul's use of the third person in describing his experience was due to more than just convention. In

---

[15] Ibid., 119.
[16] Furnish, *II Corinthians*, 545.

distancing himself from his ecstatic experience, he is more easily able to point out that this experience is not what he is using as his claim to apostolic credentials. He points out, however, that if he wished to boast about his experience, it would not be foolish because he is "telling the truth" (v. 6). His reason for not boasting is that he believes the only thing an apostle should be judged upon is what his followers see and hear. He does not want the Corinthians to judge his credentials solely on the "abundance of revelations" (v. 7a). This is probably in direct opposition to the claims his opponents are making.

Paul's "thorn in the flesh" (verses 7b–9a)

Based on the perceived value of his revelations, Paul explains how God has prevented him from becoming too "elated." In the Greek, Paul refers to a *skolops tē sarki*, which has been variously translated as a stake, thorn, or other pointed instrument in his flesh. This could perhaps be equated with our expression "pain in the neck" if it is in fact a reference to his opponents.[17] Other possibilities have been suggested to explain what Paul meant by his "thorn in the flesh," including diseases, debilities, and spiritual torments,[18] but none of these seems to fit into the context from which Paul is speaking in this section. The main problem I see with these other possibilities is that Paul also describes his "thorn" as "an angel [or "messenger," NRSV] of Satan," which seems to be much too personified to be describing a sickness. In comparing Paul's writing to writings discovered at Qumran, Michael Barré makes a convincing argument for the identification of Paul's distress with his adversaries. His conclusion is that

> the "thorn in the flesh" and the "messenger of Satan" must allude to adversaries of Paul, not to an illness, debility, or any of the other innumerable suggested interpretations of these expressions.[19]

---

[17] Belleville, *2 Corinthians*, 305.

[18] See Furnish, *II Corinthians*, 547–50 for a detailed discussion of the issue.

[19] Barré, " 'Weakness,' " 225.

Paul's description of his affliction makes it clear that it has been given to him by the Lord to keep him from becoming too elated. But this is not the only reason. Paul also makes it explicit that his "thorn" is there so that God's power can be made manifest in his weakness. Although Paul "begged the Lord about this" three times in his desire to have the persecution removed, it is likely that in this instance he is describing a different kind of experience from the one described in 12:2–4. As Furnish points out:

> It is surely unwarranted to fuse this account with the preceding report of a heavenly journey, and to suppose that these petitions were addressed to the enthroned Lord as Paul stood before him in Paradise (so R. M. Price 1980:37), for the apostle has already said that what he heard there he was forbidden to repeat (v. 4).[20]

The reason for asking three times has also been variously discussed, but I find that the explanation that makes the most sense to me is found in the footnotes to *The Catholic Study Bible* (NAB) that describe his prayer as "incessant."

Paul does not get the response he desires, that his "thorn" be removed. Instead he is told by the Lord that "my grace is sufficient for you, for power is made perfect in weakness" (v. 9). The implication seems to be that the Lord will not remove Paul's affliction, but will provide the grace to bear it. Also, it becomes apparent that God's power becomes manifest (perfect) only when the recipient is "weak" or perhaps not self-reliant. Barré seems to offer the most adequate description of this thought process in his translation, "My grace is enough for you; for (my) power is accomplished through (your) weakness/persecution."

Final boasting of weakness (vv. 9b–10)

In the final section of this passage, Paul once again returns to the topic of boasting, but only to boast of his weaknesses. This boasting, however, is different from the kind in which his opponents have been indulging. Rather than boasting solely about his credentials as an apostle, Paul prefers to

---

[20] Furnish, *II Corinthians*, 550.

boast of his weaknesses so that Christ's power will "dwell with" him (v. 9b). It is doubtful that Paul means that weakness is necessary for God's power to be made manifest. Rather, for Paul, personal weakness is the true sign of being an apostle. He is not happy about his weaknesses, but he is "content with" them if they are for "the sake of Christ." Gerald O'Collins summarizes this well:

> "Weakness" constitutes a special mark of apostolic "service." Paul's work of preaching the gospel must not, of course, be interpreted apart from his Christology. The understanding of the crucifixion as the event in which Christ proved radically "weak" forms the background to Paul's whole discussion. In the case of the crucifixion and resurrection, weakness and power constitute an inseparable unity. By raising Christ, God's power was effective and manifested in the face of that ultimate "weakness" which the crucifixion meant. In its turn the apostolic ministry undertaken on Christ's behalf involves participation in this weakness and power of Calvary and Easter. . . . Our passage may be paraphrased as follows: The power which is both effective and manifested in the resurrection of the crucified Christ reaches its fulfillment for the apostle (not in ecstatic experiences but) in diverse "weaknesses." When in this sense the apostle becomes and appears weak, he is in fact strong, effective in his ministry (cf. 10:4).[21]

SYNTHESIS

What is required of the would-be apostle? That is the question that Paul is addressing in this passage. His opponents apparently feel that it is personal charism and rhetorical skill. Paul's definition is much simpler—to be an apostle, one must be weak. Paul avoids the temptation to argue for his status as an apostle from his ecstatic experiences. Instead he relies on the Corinthians to recognize that his appearance and deeds are the things upon which he wishes to be judged. Paul's demand is that apostles be those through whom others are able to see the power of God manifested in the world.

---

[21] Gerald G. O'Collins, "Power Made Perfect in Weakness: 2 Cor 12:9–10," *Catholic Biblical Quarterly* 33 (1971): 532–33.

2 Corinthians 12:1–10 Today

To what areas of our life today can this passage speak? I will suggest three ways. First, it can speak to each of us whenever we are tempted to be too self-reliant. Second, it can speak to the ways each of us manifest apostolic activity in our own particular circumstances. Finally, it can speak to issues of pain and suffering. I will discuss each of these issues in turn.

First, there is often the potential for each of us to become overly self-reliant. Any time we begin to lose sight of the fact that our abilities are free gifts from God, we begin to miss the mark. This seems to have been the situation that Paul was addressing at Corinth. His opponents were boasting about their great accomplishments and belittling Paul's appearance and rhetorical skill. Paul used the irony of his argument to show them that in apparently building themselves up, they were tearing the church down. Paul's message reminds each of us that even if we are able to boast about our abilities, it accomplishes little. Praising our own gifts does nothing to build up Christ's Church here on earth. Rather, by using our gifts wisely, we help build up the Christian community, and thus allow the power of the Lord to be seen.

Second, we must each be conscious of how we manifest our own apostolic activity. "My power is made perfect in your weakness" has a great deal of meaning for each of us in our apostolic calling. Is Paul's message that we must actively seek out opportunities to be persecuted, belittled, or injured in order to be faithful to the apostolic mission? Not in the least. But neither does it state that we should avoid those circumstances if they arise. We must each remember that being "weak" means being in conformity to Christ. It is this "cruciformity"[22] that becomes the true sign of apostolic ministry. The Church ultimately belongs to Christ who

---

[22] I borrow this term from Michael J. Gorman and his forthcoming book *Cruciformity: Paul's Narrative Spirituality of the Cross* (Grand Rapids: Eerdmans).

founded it, not to its members as individuals. Being "weak" can be as simple as seeking counsel from God through prayer, or as complicated as enduring the hardships Paul describes in his letter. This "cruciformity" of lifestyle gives a whole different meaning and emphasis to the idea of living the gospel and spreading it.

Third, and perhaps most importantly, this passage speaks to issues of pain and suffering in our lives. In 2 Corinthians 12:10 Paul states that he is "content with" numerous sufferings that he has had to undergo for the sake of Christ. This is an attitude that can be adopted by any Christian in any life circumstance. Paul is not attempting to understand why he needs to suffer, only to accept that it must happen. Is he happy about it? Apparently not, because he asks God to remove it from him. God's reply is the one that we can each find personally comforting in our time of need—"my grace is sufficient for you." God's promise is not that following his will or that life in general will be easy or free from difficulties. He has always promised, however, to be with us throughout our turmoil. Paul is reminding his readers and his opponents that the power of God is manifested in the difficulties he faces. By uniting our own personal pain and suffering to those of Christ, we are exercising a "cruciform" spirit.

Do we today see examples of the same type of problems Paul faced in Corinth? I would argue that we see them almost daily. Wherever people forget that God is the giver of all of our abilities and gifts, the same attitude that Paul was addressing is alive and well. Any time that persons claim authority because of the gifts they possess instead of as a result of God's power working through them the same is true. People daily suffer hardships while trying to spread the gospel message to others. What must we do? The response Paul would undoubtedly give would be to remember that to be weak in the eyes of the world is to be effective in Christian ministry. Being in conformity with the death and resurrection of Christ is not an easy task, but it is the one sure way to know we are leading a truly Christian life.

BIBLIOGRAPHY

Barré, Michael L., "Qumran and the 'Weakness' of Paul." *Catholic Biblical Quarterly* 42 (1980): 216–27.

Belleville, Linda L., *2 Corinthians.* IVP New Testament Commentary Series, vol. 8. Downers Grove, Ill.: InterVarsity, 1996.

Brown, Raymond E. *An Introduction to the New Testament.* New York: Doubleday, 1997.

Furnish, Victor Paul, *II Corinthians: Translation, Introduction, Notes and Commentary.* Anchor Bible, vol. 32A. New York: Doubleday, 1984.

Getty, Mary Ann, "Paul and His Writings," RG [reading guide] 470–RG 540. In Donald Senior, ed., *The Catholic Study Bible.* New York: Oxford University Press, 1990.

Gorman, Michael J. *Cruciformity: Paul's Narrative Spirituality of the Cross.* Grand Rapids: Eerdmans, forthcoming.

Martin, Ralph P. *2 Corinthians.* Word Biblical Commentary, vol. 40. Waco, Tex.: Word, 1986.

Murphy-O'Connor, Jerome, O.P., *The Theology of the Second Letter to the Corinthians.* New Testament Theology. Cambridge: Cambridge University Press, 1991.

O'Collins, Gerald G. "Power Made Perfect in Weakness: 2 Cor 12:9–10." *Catholic Biblical Quarterly* 33 (1971): 528–37.

Sumney, Jerry L. *Identifying Paul's Opponents: The Question of Method in 2 Corinthians.* Journal for the Study of the New Testament Supplement Series, vol. 40. Sheffield, England: JSOT Press, 1990.

Tabor, James D. *Things Unutterable: Paul's Ascent to Paradise in Its Greco-Roman, Judaic, and Early Christian Contexts.* Studies in Judaism. Lanham, Md.: University Press of America, 1986.

Selected Internet Resources for Biblical Studies

The technology of the day has affected the reading, study, and distribution of the Bible since the time of its writing. In our own era the advent of the Internet has made many resources for biblical study available "online." As in every other field of study, the quality of those online resources varies considerably even as the quantity seems to grow exponentially. Listed below are a few Internet sites that seem to have established themselves as reliable, multipurpose online resources by virtue of their being produced or hosted by educational or other scholarly institutions, recognized scholars working independently, or reputable religious bodies. The focus here is on sites where the biblical text is available and on "gateways," or sites with links to other resources.[1]

For further reference, see also:

> Durusau, Patrick. *High Places in Cyberspace: A Guide to Biblical and Religious Studies, Classics, and Archaeological Resources on the Internet.* 2d ed. Atlanta: Scholars, 1998. Provides the URLs for about one thousand sites, as well as the URL for a site that lists changes to URLs, new sites, etc.

---

[1] Note: The URL ("address") for each site is given. When available, the "PURL" is also provided. A PURL is a Persistent Uniform Resource Locator. A PURL functions like a URL, but it points to a "middle man" instead of directly to the Internet resource. Unlike URLs, a PURL does not change. The PURL project is sponsored by OCLC, the Online Computer Library Center, the leader in library information services. More information is available at http://purl.org.

The Bible Online

Many searchable versions of the Bible (KJV, NIV, NASB, RSV, and more, including other languages) may be found at: http://bible.gospelcom.net/bible

The KJV, NASB, NLT, NRSV, TEV, and others may be found at a site operated by Goshen College: http://www.biblestudytools.net

Biola University runs a site with the KJV, NASB, Greek NT, and a transliterated Hebrew text at: http://unbound.biola.edu

The New American Bible may be found at: http://www.nccbuscc.org/nab/bible

The Electronic New Testament Manuscripts Project began in 1995 to make images and transcriptions of New Testament manuscripts available without charge: http://www.entmp.org

"Freeware" for Bible scholars is available in Windows and Macintosh formats for the KJV, ASV, *BHS*, the Westcott-Hort edition of the Greek New Testament, the JPS *Tanakh, Strong's Concordance*, and more from the Online Bible at: http://www.onlinebible.org/main_uk.html

The Divinity School at Vanderbilt has constructed a site containing the NRSV texts for all Sundays of the three-year common lectionary: http://divinity.library.vanderbilt.edu/lectionary

Gateways to Resources

A gateway is an Internet site with links to other sites. Among the most important of these for biblical studies are included here.

The "All-in-One Biblical Resources Search," produced by Dr. Mark Goodacre of the University of Birmingham in England, includes excellent links to Bible texts and resources, most of which can be searched from Goodacre's site: http://www.bham.ac.uk/theology/goodacre/multibib.htm

The New Testament Gateway, and the Greek New Testament Gateway, also produced by Dr. Mark Goodacre of the University of Birmingham in England, provide regularly updated, annotated links to many good academic New Testament web resources. http://www.ntgateway.com and http://www.ntgateway.com/greek.htm

Professor Terry Seland of Norway's Volda University College operates a site that focuses on the early Christian writings and their social world, with many links to texts, electronically published scholarly work, and more: http://www.hivolda.no/asf/kkf/rel-stud.html

The Faculty of Religious Studies at McGill University in Canada also has a page of links for "Bibles and Tools for Biblical Studies": http://www.mcgill.ca/religion/link-bib.htm

The College of St. Benedict and St. John's University also has a page of links for biblical studies: http://www.csbsju.edu/library/internet/theosson.html

Eastern Baptist Theological Seminary has a page of Bible-related links that includes links to software-company sites as well as other resources: http://www.ebts.edu/res-bible.htm

The Goshen College-managed site mentioned above includes not only versions of the Bible but also links to many other resources: http://bible.gospelcom.net/bible

"Offline," a column about computers and religious studies published since 1984 in several scholarly outlets, is dedicated to providing "readers with information related to computers and their use that will help them in the classroom, study, or parish." All issues are now available, with hyperlinks to all sites discussed, at: http://rosetta.atla-certr.org/CERTR/Offline/offline.html and PURL: http://purl.org/CERTR/Offline/offline.html

The Society of Biblical Literature has a section of its site devoted to electronic resources for biblical studies: http://www.sbl-site.org/Publications/E-resources/e-resources.html

The Wabash Center Guide to Internet Resources for Teaching and Learning in Theology and Religion, at Wabash College, may be found at: http://www.wabashcenter.wabash.edu/Internet/front.htm

The American Theological Library Association (ATLA) Center for Electronic Resources in Theology and Religion may be found at: http://rosetta.atla-certr.org/CERTR/CERTR.html and PURL: http://purl.org/CERTR

The Perseus Project at Tufts University permits access to searchable ancient Greek and Latin texts and to the Liddell-Scott-Jones lexicon of classical Greek: http://hydra.perseus.tufts.edu/Texts.html
LSJ lexicon: http://www.perseus.tufts.edu/cgi-bin/resolveform

Journals

Some journals that are available in print versions are, or will be, available also online. In addition, a growing number of electronic journals can be expected. Many of these will be available through the Association of Peer-Reviewed Electronic Journals in Religion: http://rosetta.atla-certr.org/apejr/apejr.html and PURL: http://purl.org/apejr

Biblica, the electronic version of the journal of the same name: http://www.bsw.org

The Journal for the Study of Rhetorical Criticism of the New Testament, sponsored by the Rhetorical New Testament Project of the Institute for Antiquity and Christianity of the Claremont Graduate School at Claremont, Calif.: http://newton.uor.edu/FacultyFolder/Hester/Journal/JSRCNTIntro.html

TC: A Journal of Biblical Textual Criticism: http://rosetta.atla-certr.org/TC/TC.html and PURL: http://purl.org/TC

Index

Actualization, 19, 22, 131, 203
Advocacy criticism/exegesis, 19, 22, 203
Ambiguity, 117–20
Antipathy, hermeneutic of, 124–25
Application, 128–29
Appreciation, hermeneutic of, 125
Approaches to exegesis, 11–22,
    195–203
Appropriation, 128–29
Assimilation, premature, 129
Atlases, Bible, 170
Authorial intention, 9

Bible
    CD-ROM, 158–60
    editions, 52–56
    interlinear, 35, 39
    study, 52–56
    translations (versions), 41–52
        for exegesis, 42–52
Bibliographies, 137–38
    resources for, 191–93

Canonical criticism/exegesis, 19, 20,
    133, 202
CD-ROM, Bibles on, 158–60
Chiasmus, 38, 82–84
Claims of text, 129–31
Close reading, 8–9, 11, 25, 33, 196–98
Commentaries, Bible, 67, 70, 136–38,
    164–65, 180–88
    in series, 183–87
    multi-volume, 183, 187
    one-volume, 164–65
    stand-alone, 183
Concordances, Bible, 174–76

Consent, hermeneutic of, 20–22,
    126–27, 202–3
Context, 24–25, 26, 30, 42, 65–73,
    96–100
    cultural, 66–69
    historical, 26, 30, 66–69
    literary, 26, 30, 69–71
    rhetorical, 69–71
    social, 66–69
Contextual analysis, 26, 30, 65–73
    resources for, 166–70
Contrast, 81
Counter-exegesis, 133
Creative fidelity, 132
Criticism, 12
    advocacy, 19, 22, 203
    canonical, 19, 20, 133, 202
    form, 15, 107, 196, 199
    historical, 15, 201
    ideological, 19, 22, 125–26, 203
    literary, 13, 196
    narrative, 13, 85–87, 111–12, 196
    redaction, 15, 107–9, 200
    rhetorical, 13, 69–71, 80–85, 197
    social-scientific, 13, 66–69, 182–83,
        198
    socio-rhetorical, 12, 183
    source, 15, 107, 200
    textual, 15, 39–40, 156, 199
    tradition, 15, 107, 200

Detailed analysis, 26, 30, 91–114
    basic questions for, 93–95
    interrelationships among parts,
        103–6
    key words and images, 96–100

phrases, sentences, text segments,
    101–3
resources for, 172–87
selectivity, 92–93
whole and parts, 95–96, 106–10
Diachronic approach, 15–17, 199–201.
    See also historical-critical method.
Diagramming, sentence, 103
Dictionaries, Bible, 67, 70, 165, 166–68
Discernment, hermeneutic of, 125

Eisegesis, 25, 128
Embodiment, 19, 22, 131–33, 203
Errors to avoid, 141–45
Etymological fallacy, 98–100
Exegesis
    advocacy, 19, 22, 203
    approaches to, 11–22, 195–203
    canonical, 133, 202
    counter-, 133
    definition of, 7–11
    liberationist, 19, 22, 126, 203
    living, 128, 131–33, 203
    paper, writing, 29–30, 205–9
    pre-modern, 21
    sample papers, 211–31
    structural, 105–6
    text for, 36–39
    theological, 19, 20–22, 126–33, 202
Existential approach, 17–22, 202–3
Expansion of the exegesis, 25, 26, 29,
    135–40, 145, 207–9
Explication de texte, 11, 14 n. 7

Form, 26, 30, 76–78, 196
Form criticism/analysis, 15, 107, 196,
    199
    resources for, 170–72
Formal analysis, 13, 26, 30, 75–90, 196,
    199
    resources for, 170–72
Formal equivalence, 43–45
Fourfold sense of Scripture, 21
Functional equivalence, 43–45

Genre analysis, 13, 76–78, 196
Grammars, biblical, 176
Grammatical analysis, 13, 197
Guessing, 61–62

Hermeneutical circle, 25, 93, 95, 103
Hermeneutics, 17 n. 11, 124–27

Historical criticism, 201
Historical linguistics, 15, 199
Historical-critical method, 15–17,
    106–9, 199–201
Horizons, 27, 127–33

Ideological criticism, 19, 22, 125–26,
    203
Illegitimate totality transfer, 98–100
Inclusio, 38, 82
Interlinear Bibles, 35, 39
Internet resources, 233–36
Interpretive postures, 124–27
Intertextuality, 109–10, 200
Introductions, biblical, 161–64

Journals, 67, 138, 179–80, 236
    online, 180, 236

Languages, biblical, 39–40
    resources for use of, 156–60, 174–79
Lectio divina, 21–22, 202
Lexical analysis, 13, 95–106, 197. *See
    also* words, analysis of.
Lexicons, biblical, 176–79
Liberationist exegesis, 19, 22, 126, 203
Linguistics, historical, 15, 199
Literary criticism, 13, 196. *See also* nar-
    rative criticism.
Living exegesis, 128, 131–33, 203
Location, reader's, 24

Method
    errors in, 141–45
    exegetical, summary of, 25–27
    historical-critical, 15–17, 106–9,
        199–201
    resources for, 148–55
Mirror reading, 68
Movement, 26, 30, 76, 79, 87–89

Narrative criticism, 13, 85–87, 111–12,
    196

Outlines of passage, 80, 144, 207

Parallelism, 81–84
Parallelomania, 110
Parallels, Bible, 157–58
Paraphrase of text, 129
Patterns, structural, 80–87
Performance of Scripture, 132, 203

Phrases, 101–3
Playing with the text, 30, 90, 113–14, 205–6
Polyvalence, 117–20
Postures, interpretive, 124–27
Pre-modern exegesis, 21
Presupposition pool, 67
Presuppositions in exegesis, 27

Reading
   close, 8–9, 11, 25, 33, 196–98
   spiritual, 19, 21–22, 202
Redaction criticism, 15, 107–9, 200
Refinement of the exegesis, 25, 26, 29, 135–40, 145, 207–9
Reflection, 26, 30, 123–34
   resources for, 188–91
Relationships among elements of texts, 103–6
Repetition, 81
Research, procedures for, 135–40, 207–8
Resources for exegesis, 147–93, 233–36
   bibliographical, 191–93
   for context, 166–70
   for detail, 172–87
   for form, 170–72
   for reflection, 188–91
   for survey, 160–65
   for synthesis, 187–88
   for task, 148–55
   for text, 155–60
   Internet, 233–36
Rhetoric, 69–71, 80–85
   ancient, 84–85
Rhetorical criticism, 13, 69–71, 80–85, 197
Ring composition, 83

Sample exegesis papers, 211–31
Scholarship, biblical, 136–38
Selectivity, 92–93
Semantic analysis, 13, 197
Sentences, 101–3, 104
   diagramming of, 103
Social-scientific criticism, 13, 66–69, 182–83, 198
Socio-rhetorical criticism, 12, 183. *See also* rhetorical criticism *and* social-scientific criticism.

Source criticism, 15, 107, 200
Sources, secondary, 29, 135–40, 147–93
Spiritual reading, 19, 21–22, 202
Structural exegesis, 105–6
Structure, 26, 30, 78–87
   expository, 84–85
   narrative, 85–87
Study Bibles, 52–56
Style for papers, 148
Survey, 26, 30, 59–63
   resources for, 160–65
Suspicion, hermeneutic of, 22, 125–26, 203
Synchronic approach, 12–14, 196–98
Syntactical analysis, 13, 101–3, 197
Synthesis, 26, 30, 115–21
   resources for, 187–88

Task of exegesis, 7–33
   resources for understanding, 148–55
Teachers, suggestions for, 4–5
Text for exegesis, 36–39
Textual criticism, 15, 39–40, 156, 199
Theological exegesis, 19, 20–22, 126–33, 202
Tools, exegetical, 136
Tradition criticism, 15, 107, 200
Translation, Bible, 40–45, 155–56
Trust, hermeneutic of. *See* consent, hermeneutic of.

Words, analysis of, 95, 96–100, 103–6
   connotation, 97, 100
   denotation, 97
   etymological fallacy, 98–100
   figurative language, 100
   illegitimate totality transfer, 98–100
   relationships among, 103–6
   semantic range, 97
Worlds and text, 17, 19, 27
Writing an exegesis paper, 29–30, 141–45, 205–9
   context, 72, 143, 206–7, 208
   detailed analysis, 144, 207, 208
   form, structure, movement, 88–89, 144, 207, 208
   introduction, 62, 143, 208
   reflection, 144–45, 207, 208
   sample, 211–31
   synthesis, 144, 207